PLAYING THE GAME
WITHOUT A COACH

PLAYING THE GAME
WITHOUT A COACH

How **Courage, Resilience, & Forgiveness**
Helped One Man **Seize** the **American Dream**

BENJAMIN RAYMOND

Playing the Game Without a Coach
How Courage, Resilience, & Forgiveness Helped One Man Seize the American Dream

By Benjamin Raymond

The events, conversations, and experiences recounted here are a compilation of my personal memories, interviews, and research. Some identifying details, including names, have been omitted or changed to protect the privacy of the individuals involved. Conversations are recorded as I recall them and are not meant to serve as a word-for-word retelling.

ISBN: 978-0-9989721-1-4 (paperback)
        978-0-9989721-0-7 (hardback)

Editor: Candice L. Davis

Published by:
Raymond Publishing, LLC
Atlanta, GA 30339

For Benjamin Troy Raymond II,
"son of my right hand" and my greatest legacy

IN GRATITUDE

To my wife, Karli. How can I ever say all that you mean to me? Your spirit, your beauty, your love, and your humor—you make me a better man every day. Thank you for the greatest gift I could have imagined, our son, BJ, and the pleasure of your friendship, support, and encouragement. I wake up every day excited to share my life with you.

To Benjamin Troy Raymond II, born on the fourth anniversary of the day I met your mother at a mentoring camp for fatherless boys. Every morning, when I open my eyes, I thank God for the privilege of being your father. Know that I love you now and for always. I look forward to accompanying you on your journey through life, and I'm sure you will do great things.

To my mother and my first love, Nancy Raymond. From the start, you've been by my side, fighting for me and for us. Thank you for teaching me to love deeply, forgive generously, and hold on to my dreams.

To my father, David "Slim" Brumfield. For so many years, I dreamed of what my life would be like with you in it. In finding you, I came to understand my own identity, and I'm proud to call to you my dad.

To Derrel Wilkerson, my stepfather. Thank you so much for all the love and care you've shown my mother and me over the years.

To Kat "Mom Kat" Hughes, my second mother. You were one of the first people to make me feel loved just for being me. Thank you for taking me in as a broken kid, for helping me become whole again, and for embracing my mother along the way.

To the Hughes family. Thank you for the gifts of discipline and structure, the security of family, and many of my best memories.

To the Schade and Nesbitt families. I am forever grateful to you all for bringing me into your homes and giving me hope.

To Davida Brumfield. At twenty-seven-years old, I discovered you, my little sister, the sibling I'd always wanted and, finally, a relative who looked like me. You and Aniah have blessed my life, and I'll always be here for both of you.

A special thank you to State Farm for the chance to represent the best insurance company in the world. That privilege has led to amazing experiences, including meeting my wife, sharing my story for the first time, expanding my mentorship, and traveling the world.

To Candice L. Davis. Thank you for grasping my vision and helping make this book a reality.

To every relative, teacher, pastor, coach, neighbor, and mentor who lent me a dollar or a hand when I needed it. And to every friend who has stood by me through the good times and the tough times. Thank you. You're all a part of the family that keeps me striving to do more, be more, and give more.

And to every intern and mentee. Because of you, and people like you, I will continue to share my story. Thank you for inspiring me to find new ways to serve.

Love,

Benjamin Raymond

FOREWORD

When I first met Ben Raymond at my mentoring camp for boys being raised by single mothers, I had no clue what this tall, athletic guy had overcome in his life. He looked like someone from an upper-middle-class background, the kind of man who grew up in a traditional family, with two professional parents, and a big old silver spoon in his mouth. I soon discovered just how far that image was from the truth. Ben's life had been anything but easy.

This was a young man who had to figure out how to define manhood on his own because the father who should have been there to show him the way was missing in action. And he had to step into that manhood at an early age because his mother's drug addiction and mental illness made it impossible for her to handle the demands of being a single parent. Ben's story was more like the stories of the boys we were reaching out to than I had imagined.

I saw a side of him few people knew at the time. He arrived as a representative of the business world, and he left as a compassionate mentor and caring big brother. Ben was so moved by his experience with our mentees that he decided to share his personal journey with them. He wanted them to realize he wasn't just talking. He really understood their pain and their sorrow, and he wanted to give them hope. I watched him comfort, motivate, and challenge a group of boys who reminded him so much of himself.

I knew he was an accomplished entrepreneur, but Ben really earned my respect as I learned about his childhood spent in and out of foster care, his love and forgiveness for the mother and father who hadn't been there when he needed them most, and his deep desire to give back wherever he sees a need. He kept showing up for the camp, from one year to the next, and he kept mentoring young men even after camp closed for the summer.

I appreciated his commitment, but that was before I knew there would be another commitment in his future—one that would make him a member of my family. If I had known he was going to end up marrying my daughter, I might have put Ben in the back somewhere at the camp, someplace where he and Karli couldn't lock eyes. Luckily, he turned out to be a great guy. If Ben wasn't my son-in-law today, I would still be proud to call him my friend.

Playing the Game without a Coach is for the little kid who wishes he could have a happy family like the ones he watches on old sitcoms, and it's for every family dealing with mental illness. It's for the teenager struggling to cope with a mother on drugs or a father locked up in America's insanely bloated prison system. It's for the man determined to make his mark in corporate America or as an entrepreneur. Regardless of the haters who tell him he's too young or too old, not smart enough or not educated enough, not the right color or the right ethnicity, he will not quit. It's for the woman who hits the glass ceiling and takes a hammer to it.

Ultimately, this book is for all of us who know—or those of us who need to know—that we create our own destiny. It's for those of us who choose to define our success not just by our own achievements but also by how much we can help other people achieve along the way. As you read it, you will be moved to tears and laughter. You'll also discover that you too have everything you need to overcome any obstacle and live the life of your dreams.

Steve Harvey

CHAPTER ONE

The man who has no imagination has no wings.
—Muhammad Ali

With fifteen seconds left in the game, I block out the thunder of the crowd and focus. *Time seems to stop as I fly down the right side of the field and drive into the end zone, catching the game-winning touchdown pass to send our rivals home defeated.*

With the win, the volume of the crowd doubles, and I bask in their admiration. It's the biggest game of the year, and as my teammates mob me in celebration, I look to the stands. My mom hugs my dad as he cheers for me, pumping his fist in the air, and even over the shouts and screams of the fans, I hear him yelling, "That's my boy! That's my son!" They never miss a game.

At home, the kitchen smells like gravy and fresh bread, and I can't wait to dive into dinner. Winning makes me hungry, but my mom never disappoints. Platters and serving bowls cover our kitchen table so there's barely room for our plates. Mom has cooked pot roast, mashed potatoes, peas and carrots, rolls, and macaroni and cheese, and she pulls pitchers of iced tea and lemonade out of a double fridge packed with food.

We all sit down together, and after my dad says grace, my parents can't stop talking about how great the game was.

My dad says, "If I was a gambling man, I would've put some money on that game."

Mom says, "If you were a gambling man, you'd have a hard time finding anybody to bet against our son," and they laugh together.

"You know," Dad tells Mom, "I showed him how to shave this morning." He winks at me.

Mom pretends to be shocked. "What? He's still my little boy!"

"Not anymore," Dad tells her. "Pretty soon, he'll be shaving every day, just in time for high school."

The three of us talk for a while about what classes I should take in ninth grade and how I'll manage sports and keep up with advanced classes. Finally, my dad looks at his watch and tells me, "Finish up and get to bed, son. You need your rest."

I talk around a mouthful of mashed potatoes and peas. "What about—?"

"Don't talk with your mouth full, Ben," my mom tells me as she slides more pot roast on my plate.

"Don't worry, son," Dad says, "we'll run those drills in the morning." Then, he turns to my mom. "Great meal, Nancy. I'll take care of the dishes."

My mother smiles at him, her blue eyes sparkling. "Ben can help you, Slim. He hasn't done any chores today."

I frown, ready to complain, but my dad lets me off the hook. "I think I can handle a few dinner dishes on my own." "Time to hit the sack, young man." He raises an eyebrow to let me know he means business, and then he gets up to stack dishes and clear the table while water fills the sink. "And son," my dad says, reaching over to squeeze my shoulder, "I'm proud of you."

They're words he's said to me so many times before, but it still makes me feel like I want to score three touchdowns instead of one in the next game.

I finish eating as quickly as I can, but before I can get out of the kitchen, my dad calls me back. "Why are your pants sagging, Ben? You want to wear those big clown pants, at least wear a belt. No son of mine is gonna walk around looking like a thug."

I like my style, but it's not worth the argument. I just say, "Yes, sir," and hold my pants up by the waist until I get out of my dad's line of sight.

Upstairs, I check my math problems twice before I close my notebook. Dad is proud of his son, the athlete, but Mom stays on top of my grades. She doesn't play around when it comes to my schoolwork.

After I turn out my light and climb into bed, I hear her come into my room. I pretend I'm already asleep, but the smell of roses on a sunny day washes over me and her hair brushes my cheek as she leans down to kiss me good night and whispers, "I love you, son."

As I drift off, I strain to hear the sounds of my dad putting away dishes, my parents talking in low voices about our next family vacation, or the two of them chuckling over a late-night talk show. But there is only silence.

The daydream was so far from my reality. But it was a way of keeping my mind occupied and shutting out the loneliness for a little while, so I went through my vision of a perfect day with my perfect family one more time as the digital clock on the VCR flipped over to 10:59 p.m. The house settled, making the kinds of noises I only heard when I was alone at night. Picturing myself leading my team to victory before a game started served me well and helped me play my best every time. But no matter how many images I conjured up, no matter how specific I got or how much I wished for it, my family life was still far from the scenes I imagined.

In reality, I sat by myself in the darkness once again, waiting for my mother to call with some excuse about why she wasn't home yet. The loneliness and isolation made me feel like I was doing time in my own home, like after school, and sports, and hanging at my friends' houses, I ended every day in solitary confinement. I wanted out.

I wasn't a typical latchkey kid, fixing myself snacks and watching TV while I waited for my mom and dad to come in after a long day at the office. My parents weren't absent because they worked lots of overtime, or traveled for work, or because a family crisis had called them away. There were no legitimate responsibilities keeping them from fulfilling their obligations as mother and father. Nothing in my life as a thirteen-year-old boy ready to start high school was quite so simple.

Six years had passed since I'd seen or heard from my father, and I had no idea where to find him, how to contact him, or whether he was alive or dead. In a room full of black men, I wouldn't be able to pick him out of the crowd. I'd last seen him when I was seven years old, but even then, I only knew he was my father because my mother said so. Until that day, he and I hadn't laid eyes on each other since I was baby. All I knew about him was what my mother's family told me— that he was a bad guy, a criminal who went to jail for robbing people.

We'd had a quick conversation on my front porch while a couple of police officers waited nearby to make sure he left without incident. After that, he was missing in action for the rest of my childhood, and I spent way too much time trying to figure out what could possibly be important enough to keep him away from his son. Was he one of those guys I saw on the news, chased down by cops, thrown to the ground, and handcuffed? Was he a fugitive on the run? Was he really as bad as they said he was?

I lived with my mother, but she'd gone out with the man she was dating, a drug dealer with a bad temper and fast hands that I prayed he wouldn't use on her that night. I assumed she was off doing what she so often did with the men in her life, partying and chasing a high that could make her forget her pain, pull her out of her depression for a while, and temporarily quiet the chatter in her head that set off her mania. When she would come home was anybody's guess.

As an only child, I didn't have sisters or brothers to share the long nights of wondering when or if Mom would make it home in one piece. We had some extended family in the area, but no one I could reach out to. And so, as I had done so many times in the past, I waited well into the night for my mother to call. With each ticking minute, the lump of anger in my throat expanded until I felt like I'd choke on the cold pizza I was picking at, and I threw it down in disgust.

I got up from the couch and walked around the house, my anger growing as I passed through each empty room. Other kids didn't live like this, and it was pissing me off that I had to sit up waiting for my mother—as if I was the parent and she was a delinquent teenager. On any given night, I could go to a friend's house and sit around the dinner table with a normal family. There'd be a real meal with food from all the food groups, and without fail, there'd be enough for seconds or even thirds. We'd talk about how our day at school was, and sports, and what we wanted to be when we grew up, and how much homework we had for the night.

But those kinds of home-cooked meals, flavored with laughter and good-natured conversation, hadn't taken place in my house in a very long time. My mother had always had her emotional ups and downs, but over the previous year, she'd spiraled down to a darker place. Her good moments were fewer and farther between, and I'd exhausted myself trying to keep her functioning and safe while doing my best to hide her deterioration from the world outside our four walls.

It was hard enough being the only black kid in the neighborhood. Being the black kid with the unstable white single mother meant I would always be different from everyone else. Even the kids on my team who had divorced parents or absent fathers had no idea what it was like to live with a mother who was in and out of psychiatric rehabilitation centers. I didn't know anyone who lived like I did, never trusting that a moment of normalcy could last. And I didn't want to live that way anymore either.

———

Earlier that evening, I made a call that would change the course of my life. My basketball coach, Frank Schade, had always said I could call him if I needed anything. "I'm going to be a rock in your life," he'd said, and I'd finally taken him up on his promise.

A combination of frustration and helplessness pushed me to dial his number, and Coach answered. "What's up, soldier?"

"Coach," I'd said, "My mom needs some help. I can't take it anymore."

Coach Schade didn't flinch. "She's going to get help," he told me. "And you can stay here as long as you need to."

It was almost like he'd been waiting for me to reach out, and he and his wife, Kris, were both ready to step in and take charge and relieve me of my burden. It helped that he'd known me and my family for several years and he saw me as more than just another player who'd soon be on his team. He'd watched my grandparents take me in whenever my mother was readmitted to the hospital. He knew she often borrowed money from team families and neighbors, always saying she needed to buy something for me. Because people liked me and loved seeing me win on the court or on the field, they were happy to help, but it didn't take long for them to figure out that money wasn't going to my needs. It was going to feed her drug habit.

My mother had used drugs to self-medicate and deal with her depression and her mania off and on since before I was born. She'd always found her way back to sobriety by getting psychiatric treatment, but recent events had pushed her into a hole she couldn't even see she'd fallen into.

Knowing some of my mother's history, Coach Schade didn't ask any questions, and I was glad he didn't pressure me for details. I was so accustomed to protecting my mother by telling people everything was all right, I couldn't have described how messed up she was.

Because I couldn't talk about it, no one really knew how bad things had gotten in our house, but the rumor mill in our small town had spread enough of the truth for Coach Schade to understand I wasn't being dramatic. I needed responsible adults to give me a way out before it was too late.

Just like her husband, Mrs. Schade had taken a special interest in me for some time. She'd gone to school with my mother, and they'd reconnected when I was in fourth grade and my mother was looking for the best Hoops Club basketball team for me to play on. Mrs. Schade recognized my mother's name, and she remembered the pretty, popular honor student she'd known in high school. The two women clicked.

Mrs. Schade's father and my mother's father had also been friends, and during my early childhood, my grandfather was the male figure looking out for my future. While I attended a nurturing private school, he knew my career in sports had to be considered in choosing my high school, and he didn't trust his daughter to make that decision alone. Not only did he have a relationship with Mrs. Schade's father, but he also recognized that Coach Schade would be a great choice to mold me as a player. Coach had played in the NBA, and he knew his Xs and Os.

Several high school coaches wanted me on their feeder teams, but the hometown connection won my mother over. Perhaps it reminded her of a simpler time in her life, a time when all of the potential in the world still lay out before her. In the end, with her father's guidance, she entrusted her son to Coach Schade and his ability to develop a player to his full potential. I joined a Hoops Club team that fed into the high school where Coach Schade ran the basketball program.

I'm not bragging when I say I was already a damn good basketball player by the time I hit eighth grade. When I started playing in fourth grade, I was like a man among boys, bigger, stronger, and faster than the other kids. I quickly became a star. In middle school, I was the one dropping thirty points and making it look easy because it actually was. By the time I finished eighth grade, I held several records, some of which would still stand when I returned to visit more than twenty years later.

Like so many teenage boys, I had my heart set on growing up to play in the NBA, where I could achieve greatness, following in the footsteps of the players I'd always admired. As a player who'd dominated on the court from the first time I held a ball in my hands, that dream felt incredibly real and achievable to me, especially since I'd proven myself in the highly competitive Amateur Athletic Union basketball league. On travel teams, like the Racine Running Rebels, I played with and against some of the best athletes in my age group, guys like Caron Butler who were also on track for pro careers. I loved picking up the paper and seeing my name in headlines like "Raymond Leads the Rebels."

I loved sports and the exhilaration of competition. On the court, I could forget about everything going wrong at home. But at the root of my NBA dreams was my long-held desire to live a better life. A childhood spent wearing other people's discarded clothes that we purchased at Goodwill, moving from house to house, and never quite having enough of anything made me want more.

The thing was, when my mother had her meds balanced out and was clean and sober, she worked hard and did her best to provide for us. She kept me active and engaged, and in some ways, I had more exposure and experiences than lots of other kids. But the reality was that, financially, we always struggled.

I wanted a different kind of life, and I was willing to work for it. I just needed a path to follow. Where I grew up, I didn't see men who looked like me starting multi-million-dollar businesses or landing C-suite jobs in major corporations. However, I could turn on the television and see Michael Jordan wearing custom-made suits and driving a black Ferrari. I saw lots of young black men earning great money playing basketball. And I wanted that money too. More importantly, I wanted the standard of living a pro ball salary could buy me. I wanted it for myself, and I wanted it for my mother. I needed to protect that dream for both of us.

My first high school basketball season would be starting in a few months, and I would be playing for Coach Schade, a coach with a winning record, at Oshkosh North High School. That decision had already been made. My destiny was tied to the destiny of the North Spartans, and I had to make the most of the opportunity.

———

When the white phone that hung on the kitchen wall finally rang, the noise shattered the stillness and startled me out of my thoughts. After so many long hours of planning and practicing exactly what I needed to say to my mother, the sound triggered a mix of fear, anger, and relief in me.

As usual, the ringing phone made my heart race with anxiety. I feared it might be bad news, that someone was calling to tell me my mother had been hospitalized again, or worse, that she'd been arrested or hurt. I was angry in advance of the lie she would tell me about what was keeping her away from home—a fake flat tire or broken-down car—and angry that she would choose whatever was out there over me. Yet, even with the fear and the anger, as soon as I answered, I was relieved, as always, to hear her voice and know she was okay.

The moment had come for me to actually have the conversation I'd had with my mother in my imagination many times over. Things were so out of order in our lives that our roles had reversed. As the child, I was placing conditions on my parent, but if I didn't take responsibility for my life, no one would. I steeled myself to say what I needed to say and walk away from the person I loved most. After she'd spoken for a moment, it was my turn.

"You know I love you, Mom," I told her, struggling to hold on to the courage it would take to get the words out. "You and me been through a lot together, and I wouldn't trade you for nothing, but today, you have to make a decision. You have to choose. It's either me or the drugs." I paced back and forth, as far as the long coiled phone cord would stretch, as I explained to her that I couldn't continue with the way we'd been living.

I didn't want to spend one more night staring out at the darkness that surrounded our house, wondering and worrying about her. During the day, I could keep myself busy watching sports on TV and playing basketball in the park. At night, as the world grew quiet, I had to contend with my thoughts, and they always centered on her self-destructive habits, her bad judgment and poor choices, and everything I was missing because she couldn't get it together.

"Mom," I said, "if I don't do this, my life is going to end up just as destructive as yours." I explained that Coach Schade and his wife had agreed to let me live with their family. I was leaving our home, and she needed to use the opportunity to get sober and healthy.

"I understand, Ben." Through her tears, my mom agreed that I should go, although she would later share with me that she also felt a certain sense of betrayal in hearing her only child give her what boiled down to an ultimatum. It devastated her to lose me to someone else's care, this time by my own choice.

As much as my mother's life seemed out of control to me, it must have felt even more so to her. She must have felt trapped by the demons of trauma and paranoia that haunted her and by the way the medicines prescribed to help her often made things worse, trapped by the physical and verbal abuse her boyfriend used to demean and control her, trapped by the lack of a place to turn to and a lack of friends who might understand and offer her a way out.

None of what I said to my mother came as a surprise to her. She knew she needed help, and she knew that until she got it, I would be better off in a more stable environment. She wanted more for me than she could give at that moment in time, and she trusted the Schades to take good care of me. She wouldn't stand in my way.

Preparing to leave our home, a part of me felt like I was abandoning my mother, the one person who had done more for me than anyone else in my life, the one person I would always defend and step up for whenever she needed me. For so long, all of my life really, it had been just the two of us. I was her right-hand guy, the one who had always been there for her, but I couldn't do it anymore.

My mother deserved so much of the credit for all of the good things I had in my life. Whatever my odds were of going pro, my basketball career was promising enough that I could clearly see a college scholarship in my future, and I would never have come that far without her support. When I was a little boy, she was the one who watched Packers games with me, took me to the park to play, and stayed out in the yard throwing the football with me long after it must have stopped being fun for her.

God had given me the physical gifts of a natural athlete, but my mother had made sure I had chance after chance to develop those gifts in soccer, baseball, football, and basketball so I could find my best fit. For much of my childhood, we were a team and I was her first priority. It hurt me to tell the woman who meant more to me than anyone else in the world that I couldn't live in her home any longer.

It crushed me to leave, but the price of staying was just too high. I thought I could handle her withdrawal into depression, her paranoid ramblings, and the grandiose ideas brought on by her mania. But her latest boyfriend had driven home for me just how bad off she was. When he came to stay in our house, he brought drugs with him, as a user and a dealer.

I'd gotten used to the smell of marijuana in the house over the years, but when I found used needles under the couch, up high in the kitchen cabinet, and behind the nightstand, I knew things had gone farther than ever before. Nobody in that house had diabetes, and the cloudy residue in those syringes wasn't insulin. Whatever he was shooting up was illegal and dangerous. It scared me to think that, with him, my mother was now using the kinds of drugs that cost people their lives.

Along with hard drugs and guns, this new boyfriend also brought violence. One day, my mother came home wearing sunglasses, obviously trying to hide her face. When I asked her what was wrong, she tried to convince me that while they were at the bowling alley, someone threw a bottle and it hit her in the face and gave her a black eye. We got into heated arguments about her outright lies, but she stuck with her story.

I could barely control the rage I felt each time I saw her boyfriend's needles or his guns laying around the house or when I laid eyes on the man I knew had laid hands on my mother. Everything in me wanted to destroy him. But he was a grown man—well over six feet tall, swoll, and mean—and even though I was big for thirteen, I was still just a boy. I couldn't fight him, but I didn't have to stand around and act like I was cool with him or the way my mother seemed to have given up on herself. As much as I wanted to tear him apart, I was also furious with my mother for failing me over and over again. I had reached my breaking point.

I wanted a life like the one I watched Theo Huxtable live on reruns of The Cosby Show. Even though it was pure fiction, I couldn't help making the comparison. He and his sisters had two sober parents, a doctor and a lawyer, who came home on time every day after work. Dr. and Mrs. Huxtable always knew where their children were and paid attention to what they were up to. The kids had curfews and rules to follow, and when they stepped out of line, their parents swooped in with swift but loving consequences. To me, it was a perfect encapsulation of the kind of life so many of my friends lived, and I couldn't understand why I didn't deserve the same thing.

Maybe I would never have those model parents I'd imagined, but I was tired of pretending things weren't as bad as they were. I was tired of finding ways to stay away from my own home whenever my mother's boyfriend was there. I was tired of pulling together snacks and cold deli sandwiches for dinner because no one had made a hot meal, and tired of trying to guess what kind of state my mother would be in when she turned up. When it came down to it, I was tired of waiting for someone else to step up and make a decision that would change my life for the better. So I made it for myself.

By the time my mother and I ended our call, I didn't know if she was really ready to fix things or if we'd ever live together again. No matter how far off track she was, she and I shared a deep mother-son bond. The thought that she might never get better tore me apart. But I also had just a little more hope than I'd had before we talked.

I hung up the phone. It was time for me to go, and I slung my bag over my shoulder and turned out the lights. As I locked the door behind me and walked away from our home, I finally cracked. The tears I'd held back broke free with a force I could no longer resist, and I let them flow.

CHAPTER TWO

If I cannot do great things, I can do small things in a great way.
—Martin Luther King Jr.

My mother, Nancy Sue Raymond, was born and raised in Beaver Dam, a town of just eight square miles, in Dodge County, Wisconsin. In 1952, when she came into the world, Beaver Dam had a population of less than fifteen thousand people, and her parents already had a son, Morrie, and a daughter, Bonnie. Their father, Lyle Raymond, was a World War II veteran and business owner who would get involved in local politics later in his life. He was a relatively big fish in their small pond. Their mother, Dolores Raymond, worked as a bookkeeper and eventually helped her husband run his business.

Nancy, the Raymonds' youngest child, was a classic all-American girl. A pretty teenager with girl-next-door looks, blonde hair and blue eyes, she won beauty pageants, made the cheerleading squad all four years of high school, and even became the captain. She was also an honor student with a bright, promising future.

By all appearances, the Raymonds were a typical middle-class family, and like many families, they spent Sundays at church. They belonged to St. Stephen's Evangelical Lutheran Church, a place of worship that was almost one hundred years old by then and which still held separate services in English and German to serve the local population. Besides the Common Table Prayer said before dinner, "Come Lord Jesus be our guest; and let these gifts to us be blessed," religion was mostly a Sunday affair in the Raymond household, but church attendance was mandatory.

Throughout her adolescence, Nancy presented an image to the world of a properly raised young lady who conformed to the expectations of society, and in many respects, that was exactly who she was. But she was also a young woman growing up in the late sixties and early seventies, a time when many young people rebelled against their parents' values, questioned what society said was right and wrong, and experimented with drugs.

Nancy came of age at a time when rock-n-roll was maturing from a genre focused on love songs and catchy tunes to songs with lyrics that made political statements and aimed to raise social awareness. She was seventeen years old in August of 1969 when Janis Joplin, Joan Baez, Jimi Hendrix, the Grateful Dead, and many of the biggest names in rock music took to the stage and performed for three days in front of over 400,000 people at Woodstock.

As a generation rebelled against convention, the buttoned-up American culture was changing, and that influence made its way to Small Town, America too. Nancy and her friends in Beaver Dam towed the line for their parents, but they also rode the wave of the larger cultural shift. They didn't make it to Woodstock, but they had their own party scene fueled by rock-n-roll and marijuana.

All of the partying didn't prevent Nancy from maintaining her grades, and she was accepted to several colleges. She chose to attend the University of Wisconsin-Madison, a large public university about an hour away from her home town, a move that would open a whole new world for her, for better and for worse.

In 1970, Nancy started her university studies with all the same promise, curiosity, and hope most students bring with them. Her first year and a half were fairly uneventful, the typical life of a college student, but that all came to an end in her third semester. In what would become a pattern she would follow for much of her young adult life, after her relationship with her boyfriend ended, she had what would have been described at that time as a nervous breakdown. A bad acid trip aggravated her fragile mental health.

Unable to function on her own at school, Nancy moved back home with her family, and her parents sought treatment for her.

As a young woman accustomed to achieving and meeting her parents' expectations, dropping out was hard on Nancy. In a family of achievers, she felt like a failure, and it fueled her depression.

After six months spent recuperating at home, Nancy's parents enrolled her in a summer program designed to help girls dealing with similar obstacles get back on their feet. It was just what she needed. The program took her away from the stress of everyday life and gave her a chance to have fun and bond with girls her age who had their own struggles. She left the program feeling stronger and more capable.

Nancy returned to the university to resume her pursuit of a degree. Back in Madison, she quickly formed fast friendships with three black girls who were also students at the university. While she felt like she was failing in the eyes of her family, her new friends accepted Nancy for who she was. It was the kind of camaraderie she'd longed for, and the support of her small circle helped her to stay on track and off drugs.

Two of these new friends were nursing students, and while she spent a lot of time hanging out and having fun, Nancy also found herself drawn to nursing. She switched from an English-Physical Education major to join her friends in pursuing a nursing degree. The healthcare path appealed to her caring, protective nature. The change of major was a perfect fit.

She had found a passion to pursue, but Nancy still had trouble managing the unstructured nature of college life. Her journey to becoming a nurse took her from school to school as she first earned her certification as a nurse's aide and finally became a Licensed Practical Nurse. In the coming years, her career in health care would have the same kinds of stops and starts.

———

My father, David Henry Brumfield, also known as Slim, grew up in the Deep South. Born in Louisiana, just a year before Nancy was born, Slim grew up between that state and neighboring Mississippi. He was the youngest of five sons, all born within a span of five years and all incredibly close to one another. Their parents, William Grant Brumfield and Flora Atkins Winnsboro, worked hard to maintain a strong family unit.

Mr. Brumfield worked for much of his life as a sharecropper, but what they lacked in wealth the family made up for in family ties and faith. No matter where they lived, parents and children attended a Baptist church together, like Mississippi Shady Grove Baptist, a small white church with an outdoor Baptismal pool and a cemetery where the Brumfield parents would one day be laid to rest.

Religion was a serious matter in the Brumfield household. Secular music had no place in their home. Instead, gospel music was the soundtrack of their life, and the boys were expected not just to attend church but to live what they learned in the sanctuary. When, one day, their father overheard the brothers laughing and joking and singing songs about letting the good times roll, he made it clear that the only good times they'd be having would be those that were church approved.

Even though money was tight, the Brumfield family often sat down to big family meals, and much of the food on the table they'd grown themselves. They raised chickens and hogs to round out meals of corn, peas, sweet potatoes, and collard greens. The boys would regularly be sent out to catch and kill a chicken for dinner. When time came to slaughter one of the hogs, their father always made sure the meat was shared with neighbors, much to the boys' irritation. Getting a meal on the table was hard work, and they weren't interested in giving any of it away.

While things were tough for the family in many ways, the brothers took full advantage of country living. They rode horses and climbed trees, swinging on tree limbs until they bent the tree to the ground. With little transportation available to them, they walked everywhere. They were physical, active boys, and sometimes that energy turned to fighting.

Mrs. Brumfield had her hands full trying to keep the boys from fighting each other, but when the Brumfield boys—William, Prentis, Edward, Ebb, and Slim—came around, anybody with good sense stayed out of their way. To fight one of them was to fight all of them, and that wasn't a good idea. By the time Slim entered high school, local schools had started to desegregate and a few white students attended Washington Parish High School. The mix meant more fights for them all.

At six-foot-three, teenage Slim was tall, but not quite as big as his oldest brother, who had him by a good four inches and had the look and build of "Mean" Joe Greene. But Slim had spent his childhood looking up to his brothers and working to match or beat their physical achievements. He might have been smaller than William, but Slim had the grace, strength, and mindset of a gifted athlete, and he excelled at basketball and baseball. In high school, he took his basketball team to the championship, and they took home the trophy. Slim was the star athlete in a family of athletes.

For the most part, the Brumfield boys became responsible, hard-working men, but for whatever reason, as he grew to be a man, Slim went down a different path from the one his older brothers took. He had done all right in school, but he was attracted to the easy money to be made with petty crimes. Just like he was a natural athlete, he was a natural-born hustler.

Slim grew marijuana for his own use and to make a little extra cash, but in the early seventies, police in Louisiana were more interested in talking to him about thefts in the area. By this time, Slim had also married a young lady, and it wasn't going well. The newlywed couple argued constantly, and she went to his father to complain that Slim had hit her. The Brumfield men didn't believe in a man putting his hands on a woman, but Slim denied that he'd done any such thing.

Between a marriage that was failing from the start and the threat of more jail time than he'd already served, Slim had more than enough reason to leave the state where he'd grown up and get out of the South altogether. He wanted a fresh start, and he left without saying goodbye to his wife.

Along with William, Slim migrated first to Beaver Dam and Reeseville, Wisconsin, small towns where they worked harvests for the food company Green Giant. In 1976, he moved to Milwaukee, where he found work with a meatpacking company. The pay was ten dollars an hour, a rate equal to more than forty dollars an hour in today's dollars. Slim's move gave him a chance to earn more money than he could back home, but it also helped him escape his troubles—at least until he could find more.

———

Initially, life was good for Slim in Milwaukee. He earned a respectable living, and his personality and charm made it easy for him to fit in wherever he went. Tall and handsome, he found himself enjoying the women on the local party scene. It was a bachelor's paradise, and he made the most of the new willingness among young women to cross racial lines in their dating lives. Even with the underlying racism of the time and place, Slim found that the city more than suited his needs.

On a cool October night in 1977, twenty-six-year-old Slim walked into John and Judy's Bar, in Beaver Dam. He struck up a conversation with the prettiest woman in the room, my mother, Nancy, who had come to the bar with her friend. After an evening of flirting, drinking, and shooting pool, Nancy climbed into her Mercury Bobcat and followed Slim back to Milwaukee, where they continued their party through the night.

A romantic relationship based as much on their love of the party lifestyle as it was on mutual attraction quickly grew between Nancy and Slim. While they both held down jobs, they both also regularly smoked marijuana and used cocaine. Slim had no idea his new girlfriend was mixing recreational drugs with the antipsychotic medication prescribed by her doctors.

Given the way people with mental illnesses were stigmatized as crazy, it wasn't a subject Nancy discussed openly. Besides, she often felt well enough that she didn't take the prescription at all. She didn't understand that was part of the cycle. Take the meds. Feel better. Find yourself in desperate need of treatment again.

As for Slim, all he knew was that he'd found a pretty girl who liked to shoot pool and hang out listening to popular Soul artists like Roberta Flack, Natalie Cole, Harold Melvin & The Blue Notes and The O'Jays with him.

While Nancy hid her mental illness from Slim, she also kept their relationship hush-hush for a while. The couple dated for almost a year before she finally introduced her new boyfriend to her family, and for good reason. Interracial relationships would have been rare to nonexistent in Beaver Dam, largely because the racial makeup of the town was almost exclusively Caucasian. I imagine my grandparents expected their daughter to come home with a college-educated, middle class, young white man. Instead, she showed up on their doorstep with a working-class, coffee-complected black man. My grandfather hated Slim on sight.

To some extent, my grandparents must have been a product of their time and place. While they hadn't lived with the kind of Jim Crow segregation that was a part of the fabric of the South, Wisconsin was by no means a bastion of racial harmony. During the 1950s and 1960s, Milwaukee was one of the most segregated cities in the nation. The public schools didn't begin a plan for desegregation until 1979, twenty-five years after the Supreme Court's Brown v. Board of Education decision declared "separate but equal" schools for black and white students to be unconstitutional, and two years after Nancy and Slim hooked up.

Would Mr. and Mrs. Raymond have been more welcoming if Slim had been a highly educated black man like Sidney Poitier in the 1967 film *Guess Who's Coming to Dinner*? Did my grandparents know or guess that Slim and Nancy spent much of their time together drinking and using drugs? Could they see a hint of the trouble under the surface of the relationship? I'll never know the answers to those questions, but I've learned that when it comes to family, race and racism are complicated matters.

Throughout their lives, my grandparents would have experienced very little interaction with people of other races. They would have had no black neighbors or friends or trusted community members. Most of what they knew about black people would have come from television and newspapers and the stereotypes perpetuated by the culture of their time. When the daughter they'd raised in a small-town, homogenous bubble showed up at the door with Slim, they must have seen him as not just an outsider but as a threat to their way of life.

The financial support her parents had provided her stopped when Nancy made it clear that she and Slim were a couple. Their party lifestyle quickly burned through much of their cash, and Nancy and Slim rarely had enough money between them to make ends meet. In spite of it all, they stayed together.

———

While Nancy had an open-minded, accepting attitude about race relations, she soon discovered that her parents weren't the only ones who hated the idea of a black man with a white woman. When she and Slim decided to move in together, they struggled to find a landlord who would rent to them. Around the country, many jurisdictions still had laws against cohabitation on the books, and the idea of unmarried couples "shacking up" still rankled many conservative people. Once they saw that Nancy planned to live with a black man, landlord after landlord slammed the door in their faces.

Slim and Nancy finally realized no one was going to rent to them as a couple. Instead of splitting up, they came up with a new plan.

Nancy went in and rented an apartment on her own, and Slim moved in without his name on the lease.

One fall day, after they'd been living together for a few months, Nancy ran into a local man, known in the neighborhood for handing out free ice cream to the kids. The two chatted, and Nancy even flirted with him a little. Finally, he asked her, "You want to go by my friends? He's got some good pot."

In Nancy's circles, there was nothing unusual about that kind of invitation. For her, the whole thing was just a bit of harmless fun, and she figured getting high was a good way to keep the fun going.

She left her car at her girlfriend's house and rode with the man to his friend's place. But when they arrived, something felt off to Nancy, and a sense of apprehension started to overtake her. Like many people do, she talked herself out of listening to that instinct. After all, she didn't want to seem weird or rude, and they had driven all the way over there. Everyone knew this guy. What could go wrong? Completely unaware of what awaited her, she decided to go along with their plan to hang out and smoke a little pot.

Inside the house, twenty-five-year-old Nancy was attacked and raped.

———

Survivors of rape are often reluctant to report the crime. In the 1970s, few jurisdictions had laws or policies in place to protect the identities of victims or shield them from being treated like the way they dressed, where they walked, or who they'd dated in the past was the real reason they were violated. Society tended to blame women for putting themselves in a position to be raped, and like many women, Nancy didn't go immediately to the police.

Instead, she returned to her friend's house. She just wanted to get her car and leave, but her friend saw the state Nancy was in. "Nancy! What happened to you?" she asked.

Nancy tried to explain it away and leave, but her friend pressed the issue. Trembling and in shock, Nancy let her story spill out to her friend, who offered her what little comfort she could.

Once she made it home, Nancy also told Slim what happened, and eventually, they reported the rape to the police. Like many victims, Nancy blamed herself. She questioned what she could have done differently, and her self-esteem all but evaporated. The rape not only destroyed her sense of self-worth, it also triggered memories of previous abuse she'd suffered and pushed her depression to new depths.

Slim blamed Nancy just as much as she blamed herself. He berated her and called her stupid for going off with a stranger in the first place. The incident drove a wedge between them at a time when the relationship had already started to show cracks. Over the previous weeks, Nancy had found phone numbers and notes from other women among Slim's things, and his long work hours only made her more suspicious. His response to the rape compounded their issues.

Nancy went back into counseling to deal with the rape, but even with therapy, she would never be able to fully process the event and move past it. Years later, she would struggle to talk about it without breaking down. It would be fair to say, that after that day, she was never the same.

While she saw a counselor, Nancy also had her prescription for Haldol, an antipsychotic medication with a long list of short-term and long-term side effects. Even though she didn't take it regularly, it was always on hand.

Whether Nancy got better or not, life went on. Slim loved to cook and entertain their friends, and their social life gradually reignited. One night, a friend opened the medicine cabinet and saw Nancy's prescription bottle. Thinking it was something that would give him a nice high, he took some of the pills. When he started to lose consciousness and foam at the mouth, Slim and Nancy rushed him to the hospital.

While the overdose incident made Slim aware that Nancy was being medicated, he had no idea what it really meant or how it would affect the two of them as the stress in their lives increased. They were isolated from their families, Slim by distance and Nancy by her parents' refusal to accept the relationship. Nancy's depression had been exacerbated by the rape and by the fact that she took her prescribed medication inconsistently. The accusations of cheating had them both on edge with suspicion. And then they added one more life-altering stress to the mix. Nancy became pregnant.

While they both looked forward to being parents, pregnancy did nothing to smooth out the relationship. As would be expected, Nancy dealt with shifting hormones, but her mood changes were exaggerated by the fact that she had stopped taking her medication because she feared it might harm the baby. Her emotional instability made it all the more difficult for her to deal with Slim's obvious cheating, and she continued to use recreational drugs.

The pregnancy was a contentious time for the couple. They argued more than ever, but they stayed together, and two years after they'd met in a Beaver Dam bar, Nancy and Slim became parents.

I was born on October 14, 1979, in Milwaukee County Hospital. Weighing in at ten pounds and three ounces, I started life bigger than most, if not all, of the newborns lying in the other bassinets in the hospital's nursery. That difference in size would continue throughout much of my childhood and would give me an advantage as an athlete for much of my life.

Slim was overjoyed to have a son, and he took great pride in giving me his name. David Henry "Slim" Brumfield named me, his firstborn child, David Antwone Brumfield. My parents went to the hospital as a couple and came home as a family with a new life for which they'd have to make room and take responsibility. Neither of them was ready for what lay ahead.

CHAPTER THREE

Never let your history control your destiny.

Slim shoved his gloved hands in his pockets and bent his head against the falling snow as he made his way down the sidewalk. The storm had gone on for hours, snow piling high in drifts, blanketing the ground, and keeping most people inside. As he approached home, Slim stopped short. Something was clearly wrong. The front door stood open in the middle of a Wisconsin winter, on a night when temperatures dipped down to the teens and twenties. The only signs of life were footprints stamped in the otherwise undisturbed sheet of whiteness.

Inside the cold, silent apartment, Slim called for Nancy, but the only answer was the echo of his own voice. As he went from room to room, Slim realized no one was home. At least, that was what he thought until he found me, his infant son, sleeping alone on their bed. "What the hell?" Slim whispered as he scooped me up in his arms.

There was no note from my mother to explain where she'd gone, no sign that anyone else had been in the house, no indication of why she'd left me behind.

My father wrapped me in a blanket and drove around town searching for my mother. As the hours rolled by, he started to give up hope that he'd ever find her. He didn't know if she'd run away or if someone had abducted her. He didn't know if someone had hurt her or she might have done something to hurt herself. She didn't have a car, so she could have been wandering lost and freezing in the snowstorm or shooting pool in a warm bar.

When he'd looked everywhere he could think to search for her, Slim finally turned to the police for help. It would be forty-eight hours before he could officially file a missing person's report on the mother of his child. Out of options, Slim gave up and took his son home.

———

Earlier that same December day, my father had awakened to find my mother standing over him, clutching a knife, and mumbling incoherently. In an act of what he called self-defense, he hit her and wrestled the knife from her. I have to think that, given his size and strength, he could have subdued her without hurting her and certainly without striking her, since by all accounts, my mother had never been a violent person. It's hard for me to imagine a situation in which a man his size would need to put his hands on a petite, meek woman like my mother.

Whatever happened in that moment, it wasn't the first time Slim put his hands on Nancy. If she said the wrong thing about him or accused him of cheating on her, he would hit her. He had a gun that he would occasionally flash to intimidate her and when he really wanted to shut her up, he would press a pillow over her face and remind her that he could stop her from breathing if he ever really wanted to.

Nancy took to wearing sweaters to hide her bruises when she went to work or out in public.

It's easy to recognize in hindsight that my mother was experiencing a manic episode and becoming paranoid. The character of her illness was such that she couldn't see the symptoms in herself, so she didn't realize her mental health was deteriorating. She didn't have the self-awareness to ask for help. As for Slim, what he saw was a jealous girlfriend who was taking things too far, and he didn't like it.

Once he had the knife, they launched into one of their increasingly frequent arguments. After the fight, my father had stormed out of the house, trusting that my mother's rage was directed at him and she would never do anything to hurt or endanger their baby.

Not long after he left, my mother also slipped out. She climbed aboard a city bus and rode around for hours with no particular destination in mind. Eventually a woman on the bus noticed her and observed that my mother's behavior was more than a little peculiar. She seemed jumpy, and she was muttering to herself about how scared she was that she was going to die. The woman made sure my mother got to the hospital. While Slim rode around the city looking for her, my mother was being admitted, yet again, for psychiatric treatment.

———

Whatever their issues were, Slim and Nancy's relationship didn't end that night she disappeared. Once social services notified him of her whereabouts, he left me with a babysitter while he visited her in the hospital. This would have been the first time he got a clear view of the hold my mother's mental illness had on her, and for someone who'd never dealt with anything like that before, it had to come as a shock.

Still, he expected that she would get better and they would go back to their everyday dysfunctional lifestyle together.

My mother did return home, less than three weeks after she'd left. She checked herself out of the hospital without finishing her treatment plan, as she had a habit of doing. Back in their Milwaukee apartment, she had no support system, and her condition quickly worsened. By January of 1980, she started to feel desperate.

Unsure of what else she could do, my mother picked up the phone and called her parents. "Please come and get me," she begged. She was afraid of what would happen to her and to me if she continued down the path she was on.

Even though they'd held their ground for some time, when their daughter called, her voice full of panic and fear, her parents didn't turn their backs on her. Instead, they promised to bring us home with them under one condition. "We'll come and get you," my grandfather told her, "but you have to promise you're not going to see that man anymore."

She made a weak attempt at negotiating, but my mother agreed to end her relationship with my father once and for all. Her parents saw him as the main reason her life was falling apart, and once she accepted their proposal, they came up with a plan.

While Slim was gone out for the night, my mother walked to a phone booth. She called her parents and told them it was safe to come and get us, since Slim wouldn't be there to try to stop them. They would need to grab me from the babysitter's place and then swing by to pick up my mother, who had packed a few things take with us.

What my grandparents found when they arrived was worse than they'd imagined. My mother was disheveled and confused and clearly not properly medicated, but of course, they'd seen her that way before. Even more shocking to them, at just three months old, I was malnourished, dehydrated, and clearly in need of care. Seeing me in that condition confirmed their deepest concerns, and they couldn't get us out of there fast enough. The four of us were gone well before Slim returned.

———

While my grandfather had nothing but animosity for my father and had no particular affection for me, my grandparents recognized that, at this point, I was one of my mother's choices that couldn't be undone. She and I were a package deal. They had to take me along with her, but they didn't have to make room in their lives for my father, and they wouldn't.

With my mother and me safely tucked away in their Beaver Dam home, my grandparents had all the decision-making power over our lives. They were in control of where my mother went, when, and with whom. They were in control of who was allowed to see her and me. And Slim wasn't on that very short list.

It wasn't hard for my father to figure out where we had gone. He knew how isolated my mother had been and that she really only had one place to go. When my grandfather drove her back to the place she and my father had shared to pick up a welfare check, Slim saw the two of them together, and it confirmed for him that my mother had run home to her parents.

Even though my grandparents had never welcomed him in their home, Slim held out hope that he could still be a part of my life. He packed up and moved to Beaver Dam too. He found a job in town, tried to start a life there, and continued his attempts to see us. Sure that his daughter's life would be better without Slim, my grandfather blocked him at every turn. My father sent me small gifts, like a stuffed bear, but it was all wasted. My grandparents wouldn't allow him near us.

In fact, he didn't allow anyone outside of the family near us. He had a half-black grandson living in their all-white community, a place with conservative, often racist, values. My grandfather was running for alderman, and it would have caused an embarrassing scandal for his young daughter, who most people in Beaver Dam remembered as a clean-cut, rule-following young lady, to show up as an unwed mother. That the child was black just added insult to injury.

Not only was I the product of my mother's unmarried relationship with a man my grandparents despised, I didn't look like them. There was no passing me off as white. Anyone could see I was a curly-haired, light-skinned, green-eyed black child, and that wasn't going to fly in their neck of the woods. Two months after we got there, they moved my mother and me out of Beaver Dam and stashed us an hour away.

———

Mentally, emotionally, and financially, my mother was in no state to direct her life. She relied on welfare and her parents to make ends meet, so when her father said we were moving, we moved. He transplanted us to Oshkosh, where we lived in Captain's Cove, a Section 8 housing complex.

My mother had no friends in the area and no visitors dropping by to spend time with her or check on how she was doing. She'd long since lost touch with the girlfriends who might have looked out for her as she adjusted to her new life. Moving to a new city separated her from a lot of the self-destructive behavior she'd participated in with Slim, but it also left her more alone than ever.

My mother struggled to find her footing, and the property manager's constant harassment didn't help. He hated seeing this young, pretty white woman with her half-black baby, and he constantly found a reason to hassle her. My mother prided herself on keeping a clean house, but he nagged her about the odor that emanated from the diaper pail where she kept the soiled cloth diapers. He was looking for reasons to get rid of her, and when he couldn't find any, he settled for hassling her every chance he got.

After having me in their home and nursing me back to health, my grandparents started to come around to having a relationship with me. The week before Easter, just about a month after we'd settled in, they showed up with Easter eggs for my mother and a cake decorated with roses and a cross. My mother had taken to calling me Ben, instead of David, and "Jesus loves you, Ben!" was written across the cake in frosting.

The surprise visit and gifts were my grandparents' way of opening their hearts to me. It was also my grandmother's way of reminding my mother that, regardless of what was going on with her, I deserved a childhood. In her isolation, my mother had grown angry with the world, and she had announced to her parents that she wasn't doing all of that Santa Claus and Easter Bunny stuff with me. Somehow, that Easter cake made her change her mind.

Unfortunately, the simple routine her parents had hoped she'd fall into after she moved to Oshkosh never quite materialized. Left to her on devices, my mother slid back into depression and her paranoia ran wild. On the first of April, she called social services to inquire about day care assistance. When the social worker visited, she thought my mother was acting strangely, but since I appeared healthy and well cared for, the social worker assumed my mother was doing okay and didn't take any action.

Five days later, on Easter night, April 6, 1980, my mother called the police. She claimed that someone had broken into our home to try to hurt both of us. The officers who arrived on the scene found her disheveled, disoriented, and irrational. They checked the windows and doors for signs of forced entry. Inside, they searched every room and in every closet, anyplace where an intruder could hide. When they asked my mother what had happened, she repeated her story, insisting that someone had broken in and meant to do us both harm.

One of the officers radioed for a social worker, while the other tried to calm my mother down. When the social worker arrived, she picked me up and wrapped me in a blanket.

"Where are you taking my son?" my mother asked.

"He'll be fine, Miss," the social worker said, and she rushed past my mother and out the door.

"Wait! Ben!" my mother screamed. "Ben!" She reached for me, but the officers held her back.

Sitting in the back of the police car, my mother stared out at the sedan the social worker had placed me in. She watched as a stranger drove away with her infant son, and her body shook with fear and heartbreak and the tears that sprung from the primal part of her that knew her child shouldn't be separated from her.

"Where are they taking my son?" she asked over and over, but no answer the officers gave could satisfy her. Her worst fear, that someone would come into our house to hurt us, was coming true.

They admitted my mother to Winnebago Mental Health Institute on a seventy-two-hour emergency detention. She would be evaluated to see whether or not she should be involuntarily held over for further treatment or released.

I was taken to foster care.

———

While my grandparents had started to come around in the way they thought about me, they didn't take me in when my mother was hospitalized. I doubt they were ready to introduce me to their friends and neighbors. Whatever their reasons were, they left me with the foster family.

My first set of foster parents lived in a brick house just a few miles away from where my mother and I had lived. At the time I was placed with them, they had three older foster kids in their care, a teenage girl, an eleven-year-old boy, and an eight-year-old girl. And then there was me, not yet walking or talking.

At the end of her three-day evaluation period, a probable cause hearing ended with a finding that my mother should be detained for another fourteen days for further treatment. Her medical records indicated that she had no ability to concentrate and was easily distracted. At first, she denied that she was hallucinating, but she wandered aimlessly around the unit talking to herself and responding to voices only she could hear. At the end of the two-week detention, my mother voluntarily extended her treatment, and my stay in foster care continued.

———

Soon after she was admitted, doctors interviewed my mother's family to get a clear picture of her struggle with mental illness over the years. They discovered my mother had been in and out of the hospital for psychiatric treatment for most of her adult life, including the short stay at Milwaukee General just a few months earlier, when she'd left me home alone, and had seen doctors for outpatient treatment off and on since her college years.

Bonnie, my mother's sister, had been her closest confidant, but according to her, once my mother started dating Slim, who they referred to by his given name, David, she withdrew from the family. Bonnie said Slim had told the family he worked as a "pool shark," and they had reason to believe he was involved in welfare fraud, insurance schemes, and other illegal activities. The many fake IDs he had didn't help his case much.

My grandparents also disclosed that Slim had called them on several occasions to ask for money, which they refused, and that they believed he beat their daughter on a regular basis. They worried that he'd dragged her into his shady ventures, including check-cashing schemes. Even though they had bailed my mother out of tough situations over the years and always welcomed her home in times of need, they said, when she showed up pregnant and unmarried, they drew a line in the sand.

They disapproved of her "illegitimate pregnancy" and her lifestyle in general, and they chose that moment to cut off all money and assistance. They admitted they had left her to have the baby on her own and figure out how to provide for her new family.

Not long after I was born, my grandparents started to doubt that decision. They worried that their daughter's situation might have declined dangerously without their help, and in a moment of compassion, they traveled to Milwaukee, where she and Slim lived. They found her destitute. My mother had little of the basic necessities and comforts. Her parents realized that if they didn't provide some assistance, things would only get worse for her, and before they left, they gave her money, food, and clothing. Although she had just delivered their grandson, my grandparents didn't ask to see me.

As for our recent move, they explained to the doctor that they had moved my mother and me to Oshkosh in hopes that she would experience less prejudice there than in Beaver Dam and that people might be more accepting of her "mulatto child."

I have to wonder if their concern was for her comfort or for their own embarrassment. The move certainly didn't protect my mother from racism. At that time, there were few places in Wisconsin or in the United States where she wouldn't have faced prejudice, and she was shunned in Oshkosh too. The looks and comments strangers gave her when she pushed me down the sidewalk in a stroller left her increasingly afraid to leave home. She was already emotionally fragile, and she couldn't face insult and humiliation day after day.

As the days passed, she stayed inside more and more, avoiding simple errands, like going to the grocery store, and falling deeper into depression. Within weeks, she would make the call to the police that landed her in Lake Winnebago.

Last, my grandparents also shared with doctors that my mother had taken to calling me by a new name. She wanted to change my full name from David Antwone Brumfield, the name she and my father had given me, to Benjamin Troy Raymond. Life for her was difficult enough as a single mother who'd never married. She imagined it would make things easier and cut down on the questions when she enrolled me in school, took me to the doctor, and did the other everyday things mothers did with their children if she and I shared the same last name.

My mother also liked the name Benjamin, a Hebrew name she'd found in the Bible. One of its meanings was "Most Beloved Son," and her parents liked that the name change would get them that much closer to erasing my father from our lives. Because I wasn't even a year old yet, the family was sure that changing my name wouldn't affect me at all. They were wrong. It would have a significant impact on my life.

———

For the first month of her hospital stay, my mother had no idea where I'd been taken. She knew I was in foster care, but her social worker couldn't tell her where I'd been placed. However, she did tell my mother there was no guarantee that the state would give me back to her. She'd have to achieve certain milestones to prove her competence first, and that started by taking her medications as prescribed. The fear that she might never see her only child again haunted and tormented my mother, and she would harbor a fear of losing me for many years to come.

As her condition improved and she became more aware of the gravity of the situation, the chance to reunite with her son motivated her to follow the plan social services laid out. If she stuck to it, it would prepare her to petition for a restoration of custody, but it would be a long process.

Once other neurological and mental health issues were ruled out, my mother was diagnosed with bipolar affective disorder. At the start of her treatment at Lake Winnebago, my mother's paranoia made her resistant to taking the drugs that were supposed to get the paranoia under control. Her doctors tested different prescriptions in increasing doses until they found the levels she needed to become coherent, rational, and stable again.

As her condition improved, my mother complied with taking her medications, but she continued to be unrealistic about her ability to live on her own and take care of a baby by herself. It took weeks for her to fully comprehend that things wouldn't be so easy. In the past, she had developed a habit of checking herself out of the hospital without completing her treatment. This time, it wasn't an option. They couldn't force her to stay, but if she left, she would be walking away from her best chance of getting me back.

Little by little, my mother worked the plan. She found a temporary job through a work program. In mid-July, she was allowed a trial run in a transitional home, otherwise known as a halfway house. She did well, and almost four months after she was admitted, my mother was discharged to transitional living. But it was only the beginning for her. She still had a steep hill to climb if she was ever going to bring me home.

CHAPTER FOUR

When you won't quit, you can't lose.

M y mother rang the doorbell and waited. Finally, an empty-handed Mrs. Miller opened the door.

"Where's Ben?" my mother asked. She squeezed the ball she'd brought for us to play with at the park.

Mrs. Miller smiled and shook her head. "He just went down for a nap," she said in a low voice. "Maybe next time?"

Forcing a smile, my mother agreed with her. "Sure. I'll get here a few minutes earlier." She bit her lip and blinked away tears as she hurried to where my grandmother waited in her car.

Once she transferred to the halfway house, my mother was finally permitted to visit me for a few hours at a time. At first, it made her hopeful about getting me back, but the visitations weren't easy. Without transportation of her own, she relied on my grandmother's availability to drive her to my foster family's home. When she got there, the time passed quickly. Before she knew it, she was handing her only child over for someone else to parent once again—assuming the visit happened at all. Too often for her, my foster mother told her I was sleeping and couldn't be disturbed.

Whether she got to see me when she showed up for a scheduled visit or not, the pain of our separation from each other threatened to drown my mother every time she had to turn and walk out the door, leaving me behind. For the short time my mother had raised me, a combination of paranoia, mania, depression, and drug use had interfered with her ability to make the most of that experience. Now that she was completely sober and her prescribed meds were at the right levels, she had more clarity than she'd enjoyed in a long time.

While her improved health made it possible for her to function in society and take care of herself, it also forced her to take a good look at exactly how far off track she'd gotten. With clear eyes, she faced the reality of the choices she'd made, and she constantly brooded on what she was missing as a consequence. I was growing up fast, learning to crawl, and walk, and talk, and I was doing it all without her. At the end of each visit, it was all she could do to get out the front door of my foster home before she broke down.

My mother agonized over the possibility that my foster parents planned to take me away from her for good. She watched them growing closer to her son with each passing week, and it disturbed her. The Millers didn't always parent the way she wanted to see me raised either. She worried about what they fed me and how much, especially since my foster mother was overweight. She worried that I would fall in love with this new family and prefer them over her. When she found out I slept in the same room with Mr. and Mrs. Miller, it set her off, and she complained to the social worker. She thought it was completely inappropriate for strangers to have me in the room with them at night, but it wasn't her call to make.

In August of 1980, when I was ten months old, my mother took me to be baptized during one of our scheduled visits. For her, it was an important exercise of her role as a mother. My grandmother, grandfather, and aunt stood next to her as the pastor welcomed me into the church. For all appearances, she was a single mother, yes, but a mother leading her son through an important time-honored Christian tradition. Except for the absence of a father, our family looked "normal," but at the end of the day, my mother still had to return me to my foster family.

Around that time, the Millers, who grew more attached to me every day, started talking about adopting me, and it terrified my mother. She had been through too much since she'd gotten pregnant with me, and especially since my birth, to lose me. She was working too hard to get me back. She couldn't stomach the idea that it might all be for nothing.

I was all she had, and the odds of winning me back weren't exactly in her favor, but she didn't give up. She found work as a home health care provider and continued to follow the social worker's plan. She also kept up her visits with me, the one thing she could do to make sure I didn't forget her and the bond we naturally shared stayed strong.

My mother passed the required drug tests with no problem because she had stopped using any kind of recreational drugs. But social workers also monitored her compliance with taking her prescribed medications, which she'd always struggled with. They required that she stay employed and find a decent place to live once she was discharged from the halfway house. She could only see me on their schedule, and the threat of having her parental rights permanently terminated followed her like a shadow no amount of light could make disappear. All of the conditions put a tremendous amount of strain on her.

By the time my first birthday came around that October, six months after my mother was taken away by police and lost custody of me, she'd received permission to take me on short outings, not far from where I lived. For my birthday, she and my grandmother took me to a local park. They presented me with a few toys to unwrap and a birthday cupcake, and they sang happy birthday to me.

At one year old, I imagine I was perfectly happy with whatever toys and treats they gave me and loved the attention the two women showered on me. However, my mother couldn't shake her thoughts of what we were missing—a party in her home with balloons and streamers; friends and family making a fuss over the birthday boy; party games and noisemakers; a single candle on a big, frosted cake with my name on it. In her eyes, our celebration of my first birthday was just a fraction of what it should have been. It was one more way she'd failed me, and she would beat herself up over it for years to come.

———

As the months passed, my grandparents softened their hardline approach to dealing with my mother as they observed the effort she was putting into rebuilding her life and her family. To help her meet the conditions set out by her social work plan, they secured a house for her to live in. As a part of our graduated visitation schedule, she earned permission to take me for short visits in her new home.

Finally, the day came when the social worker assigned to our case would make a final determination about my custody. The three of us went to a local park, and my mother and I played on the playground and shared a snack. My mother wasn't one to sit on a bench while I played alone. She was hands on, and I was accustomed to having fun with her in our time together. Anyone watching us could see how much we loved each other.

The social worker was moved by the way I held onto my mother and wrapped my arms around her neck. "This little boy belongs with his mom," she told my mother at the end of the visit, "and I'm going to make that happen."

It did happen. After almost two years, my mother's rights were restored, and we were reunited. My mother was overjoyed, but even more, she was relieved. A long, trying stage of her life had come to a happy ending. My grandparents were proud of her accomplishment. For the first time in a very long time, their younger daughter had set a long-term goal, followed a plan over many months, and achieved what she set out to do.

When it was time for me to transition back to my mother's care, my foster parents took me to my mother's house. "This is your new home, Ben," they explained as they handed me over to my mother. She kept Mrs. Miller up to date on my adjustment for the next few weeks, but after so much time apart, my mother really wanted the two of us to be a normal family unit for the first time. The relationship with my former foster family eventually died out, and for the time being, my mother was the only parent in my life.

CHAPTER FIVE

*The difference between the impossible and the possi-
ble lies in a person's determination. —Tommy Lasorda*

I was the center of my mother's world after she got me back, and she
threw herself into giving me everything the best life she could. While
she had little money, with her parents' help, she found ways to give
me the best childhood she could provide. She still had to contend
with dirty looks and nasty comments when some people saw her with
her little black son. Strangers shook their heads in dismay, and one
woman asked, "Well, why'd you have him in the first place, slut?"
when she saw my mother scolding me in the aisle of a grocery store.

The racism wasn't going to go away. For many people in the small,
almost all-white town of Oshkosh, Wisconsin, bringing a biracial
child into the world went against their most basic values. The way
they saw it, my mother deserved to be shunned for getting involved
with a black man in the first place. But over time, other people got
used to seeing the two of us together and either accepted it or decided
to tolerate it without comment.

Our home on High Street was near the University of Wisconsin-Oshkosh, and there were lots of students who threw the stereotypical out-of-control parties. On weekends, intoxicated coeds ran around half-dressed, laughing and leaning on each other as they walked down the sidewalks, and drunk frat boys stumbled around acting like downing half a keg of beer was the most fun they'd ever had. There were also lots of families in our neighborhood, and kids ran up and down the wide sidewalks and from yard to yard and house to house.

Together, my mother and I settled into an awkward acceptance of a world which was peppered with moments of racism directed at one or both of us. In Head Start, a preschool program for low-income families, there were a couple of other black kids. I can't recall if they were picked on too, but older white kids targeted me. They'd knock over my blocks, shove me, and call me "nigger boy." I didn't know what the word meant, but the underlying message was clear. I wasn't one of them, and they didn't want me around. The hatred behind their actions and words stung and made me afraid of what they might do next. School became a scary place, where, with each passing day, I became a little more aware that I was never going to fit in.

As my time in preschool went on, my mother noticed my behavior changing for the worse. Rather than coming home at the end of the day bubbling with excitement and eager to tell her everything I'd done and learned, I'd come home from school withdrawn and sad. I'd sit at the kitchen table and quietly wolf down my after-school snacks. At that age, I couldn't fully articulate what I was experiencing or how it made me feel, but my mother could see there was a problem. She started searching for a better school environment for me.

Outside of school hours, I spent most of my free time riding my Big Wheel with my friends or at the park with my mom. I loved to play with the three Asian boys who lived in my neighborhood. Because we spent so much time together, even now as a grown man, I remember their names: Kai, Kanai, and Koo. At that age, I was too busy having fun to worry about their different-sounding names or why they didn't look like everyone else either.

Wisconsin was a state where more than ninety percent of the population was white. Less than five percent of Wisconsin residents were black and even fewer were Asian. Just like me, my three Hmong friends, with their straight, dark hair and skin the same perpetual tan as mine stood out among the pale-skinned majority. The four of us naturally gravitated to each other, and we played at each other's houses or out in the neighborhood with our toy cars and motorcycles, bikes and Big Wheels, or action figures.

In spite of the struggles at school, I was thriving, and my mother was doing well too. Her mental health was the best it had been since she left home for college ten years earlier. She'd taken a break from dating and focused all of her attention on raising me. She was no longer abusing drugs, and for the most part, she maintained consistent use of her prescribed medications. But she still struggled at times.

Throughout most of my childhood, my mother still smoked marijuana, and depending on the company she kept, she used other drugs too. Just as I was getting old enough to start school, my mother started dating again, and her choice of men was never good. If she dated a man who abused cocaine, then she used cocaine too. Inevitably, the relationship would run its course, and when it ended, my mother would suffer another breakdown.

Whenever that darkness threatened to swallow her again, she went back into the hospital and I went back to my grandparents. Holidays continued to be incredibly difficult for her. Every year, Easter,

Thanksgiving, and especially Christmas would trigger a setback in her mental illness, and she'd go away again.

Because of that routine, I spent almost every holiday at my grandparents' home. Aunt Bonnie's two children also came to visit, so I always had someone to play with, and we had fun. My grandparents had come to accept me and treat me with the same kindness and love they showed their other grandchildren, and I had no memories of them treating me any other way. We all enjoyed our time together.

That kind of family gathering at the holidays should have been a tradition to look forward to, but the emptiness I felt at my mother's absence robbed those days of the joy they should have had. For me, there was a hole no one else could fill, and even though our grandparents kept us busy, I never stopped missing her.

I couldn't understand why my cousins had two parents who doted over them, helped them decorate the Christmas tree and wrap gifts, and made sure they got whatever special toy they wanted for Christmas, and neither my father nor my mother could find a way to spend just one holiday with me. I learned, at an early age, to pretend to be happy so no one would feel bad for me or ask me what was wrong. I didn't want pity, and I didn't want to ruin things for everyone else. My mother's holiday setbacks and my pretending they didn't matter formed a routine that would last into my adulthood.

One day, during my fourth Christmas, my mom called from the hospital to talk to me. "Guess what, Ben," she said. "I'm getting you a dog for Christmas!"

I said okay and pretended to be excited, but in my heart, I had my doubts. It seemed too good to be true. I figured she was telling me that to make me and herself feel better. By the time she came home, she would have forgotten all about it or she'd have a million reasons why a dog wasn't a good idea.

When my mother was finally discharged, my grandparents took me back home to her. My mother called me out into the backyard. "I want to show you something," she said.

She introduced me to the dog she'd gotten for me. It was a German shepherd-collie mix my mother adopted from the Humane Society. "She's yours," my mother said. "You can name her anything you want."

I stood there, wide eyed. I couldn't believe such a big promise had come through. "Mine for real?" I asked.

"For real," my mother said. "Didn't I promise you I'd get you a dog for Christmas?"

I unfroze my little feet, ran out on the grass, and threw myself at the black-and-brown dog. I hugged her and petted her while she jumped on me and licked my face until we were both rolling on the ground, and I was laughing uncontrollably.

I named her Lady, and from that point on, she was my constant companion. My mother had chosen wisely when she picked a bigger, stronger dog. I was so delighted to have a dog of my own that I'd grab Lady and practically hang from her neck. I was a little rough, but it was all out of my devotion to my dog. It was the best gift my mother could've gotten me and a reminder that, sometimes, promises are actually kept.

─────

When it was time for me to go to kindergarten, my mother chose to send me to Grace Lutheran School. Tuition was charged on a sliding scale based on household income, and what little she owed, my grandfather covered for her. The decision turned out to be one of the best she could have made for me. The small private school provided me with a safer, more nurturing environment.

From the beginning, the teachers and administrators took me into their fold. They certainly weren't used to having black kids in the school, but I was a good kid who wanted to please the adults around me. I almost always had a smile on my face, and my teachers responded to my friendliness and my enthusiasm. They seemed to treat me the same way they treated everyone else. It was as close as we could hope for to an environment that would allow me to grow and learn like the other kids. It didn't hurt that I had a huge crush on Ms. Eichman, my kindergarten teacher, either.

When I wasn't in school, my mother kept me active and involved. I was a high-energy kid, and sports provided a natural outlet for me. After school, I went to the YMCA every day. It was great for my mother because the pastor from school would drive me there when she had to work or didn't have transportation—just one of many ways Grace Lutheran provided a safety net for our family. It was great for me because there was always something to do, and I was happy to play any game or try any sport or activity.

The Y became a safe haven for me in those early childhood years. I watched older kids playing basketball, and I wanted to do what they did and be as good as they were. Older athletes acknowledged me and encouraged me, and it was just a fun place to be. By first grade I was beginning to learn the ins and outs of different sports, and by second grade, I was playing on organized teams and attending sports camps at the university.

That university camps were special for me because I'd see more young black men there than I did anywhere else. They gave me the male attention I craved, especially after they saw how well I did at whatever sport they put me in. In later years, one young college ball player, ET, would take a strong liking to me. He was a talented player, and provided me with some of the attention I craved from an older black, male role model. His attention made me want to work even harder to be the best.

I loved running, and jumping, and climbing. I loved competing, but mostly, I loved to win and the way people praised me and celebrated with me when I did. Whenever I went outside to play, I always had a bat, a ball, or a glove with me. I was always taller than the other kids my age, but where some bigger kids were awkward with their extra size, I was fortunate enough to have speed, coordination and a genuine love of the fun of the game—almost any game—that all came together to make my height an advantage.

By second grade, I was trying almost every popular sport. I joined the Mat Rats wrestling team. As a young wrestler, I wasn't always the strongest, but I was quick and gritty. I won my matches and ended the season in first place. I also ran track, and tried baseball, and played football, basketball, and soccer. I was a huge Packers fan, and my mother and I watched all the games together. On every commercial break, I'd drag her outside to throw the football with me. It was great having a mom who loved sports too. She could throw a ball and shoot a basket, but she must have been thrilled when I started playing organized sports and had practice to go to and games to focus on.

———

For several of those formative years, my mother and I had a relatively quiet life. We didn't have much in the way of material things, but we had enough. We shopped for clothes at Goodwill and bought whatever food items were on sale, but I had my bike, and I had my Legos and my action figures, including ThunderCats and my favorite wrestlers like Hulk Hogan and the Ultimate Warrior. My mother was hands-on with me. She took me to Menominee Park Zoo on Lake Winnebago, where we paid ten cents for food to feed the lambs, the baby goats, and the peacocks. It wasn't a life of riches, but my mother and I had a wealth of fun together.

One day our fun was interrupted by an unexpected, and as far as my mother was concerned, unwanted, visitor. I was seven years old, and completely unaware of the significance of the ringing doorbell. My mother went to answer it, and she spoke to a man through the locked screen door. As they talked, her voice grew high-pitched with emotion.

"You can't come in," my mother firmly told him. "Leave, or I'm calling the police." Finally, she shut the door, picked up the phone, and called the police as she had threatened. She told them a man she was afraid of, a man who had hurt her in the past, was standing on her front porch and wouldn't leave.

Within minutes, a squad car pulled up in front of our house. Two officers got out and approached the man, but he didn't run from them. "I just want to see my boy. I haven't seen him in years," he told them.

After a short conversation, the officers gave in to his plea. One of them knocked on our door and talked with my mother. They all agreed the man could sit and talk with me on the front porch for a few minutes, but then he would have to leave.

My mother's voice trembled as she called me to the front door. "Ben," she said, "there's someone here to see you. This is your father, Ben." She opened the screen door and nudged me outside.

I was in awe of the tall, broad-shouldered, brown-skinned man who stood in front of me. I had always been curious about who my father was and what he looked like. Did I look like him? Did I talk or walk like him? Did we have the same laugh? Was I a little mirror image of my father the way so many of the boys in my school looked like smaller versions of their dads? Now he was standing right in front of me, and the only reason I knew it was him was because my mother said so.

Over the years, I'd asked my mother and her parents about my father and why he wasn't around, and they'd told me he was a bad guy. Shortly after I was born, Slim had robbed a jewelry store, they explained, and he'd gone to jail for it. They told me he was a drug dealer and lifelong criminal. "Sure he loves you," my grandfather had said, "but he just can't stay out of trouble."

My father reached out and touched my head with his wide hand, as if he needed to make sure I was real. "It's good to see you, son," he said.

The policemen stood next to their squad car, keeping their distance, but still present and ready if they were needed. I wondered if they were waiting to take him back to jail. "I heard you robbed a bank," I told my father. My head was so full of those "bad guy" stories. They were all I could think of as I sat next to him, but I was more curious than scared.

He shook his head. "No, son," that's not true," he explained. "I did steal some jewelry. I got charged for that. But robbery means you use a gun or try to hurt somebody when you take something, and your daddy never did that." He handed me a small teddy bear. "I love you, son. Yes, I've done some bad things, but I never forgot about you. I always wanted to see you."

I didn't know what to say, so I sat there clutching the stuffed bear, the first gift my father had ever given me. Finally, with a little prodding from him, I told my father how much I liked playing soccer and basketball, and he lit up. He loved sports when he was a boy too, he told me.

The sun started to set, and my mother stuck her head out the door. One of the policemen waved at this man I'd imagined meeting so many times. It had been six years since he had last seen me, and now, suddenly the conversation was over.

After my father left, I thought of all the questions I wished I'd asked him and the things I wished I'd told him about. Over the years, as I grew up, the questions would multiply, and the things I wanted to say to him would grow harsher. I would long for another opportunity to see him and ask him everything I wanted to know, but didn't have the presence of mind to ask at seven years old. I would long to tell him how he hurt me when he went away, how much I needed him, and why I didn't need him at all.

I was glad we had that brief moment together, but it would be the last bit of my childhood I shared with my father. When he left, he was gone for good.

No matter what sport I was playing, my mother made sure I made every practice, and she showed up to every game. On the field, or the court, or the track, I didn't have to worry about fitting in. Every sport I tried came naturally to me. No one cared what my hair texture felt like or how big my lips were when I helped my team win.

From second grade on, playing basketball at Grace Lutheran, I was like a man among boys on the court. I had a natural agility, coordination, and speed, which I would later learn I'd inherited from my father and his family. Those gifts, handed down from father to son, and constant practice made it easy for me to shine on the court.

While my father provided the right DNA for me to develop as an athlete, my mother did her part too. With her parents' support she found the best teams and summer camps to help me develop my athletic abilities. Her commitment to giving me these opportunities not only made it easier for me to build friendships, it set me on a course that would help me develop the skills I'd need to be successful for the rest of my life in academics, corporate America, philanthropy and service, entrepreneurship, and ultimately, family and relationships.

Sports gave me the structure I lacked at home and the discipline and accountability of practice, showing up on time, learning a playbook, and being a team player. These gifts would be honed in me over years of playing different sports on different teams, especially in football and basketball. I would always be grateful to my mother for making sure I had access to any and every opportunity to develop as an athlete.

Although soccer wouldn't turn out to be my favorite sport, playing the game provided me with an unforgettable experience—my first thrill of victory. In third grade, I played in my first real soccer game. I was fast, and I loved running. There were orange slices and snacks waiting for us on the sidelines, and our parents were there cheering for us. We were just little kids, but it felt like an important event. By the end of the game, I'd scored three goals.

My whole team and everyone who'd come to see us play went wild. They shouted my name and told me what a great job I'd done. Random parents came up and gave me high-fives. As a little kid who'd really struggled to fit in and feel like I belonged, it was an incredible day. I had done a great job, and people admired me for it. I was too young to distinguish their appreciation of my performance from a love for me, a little boy named Ben, but for the time being, it didn't matter. I'd felt the high of winning, and it was a feeling that would fuel my drive to be the best for years to come.

———

I enjoyed soccer, but I loved basketball even more. In fourth grade, I joined Hoops Club, a youth league that would challenge and stretch me as a player in new ways. That year, the team planned a trip to Arizona for the players and our families. A trip like that should have been out of reach for someone in my mother's financial circumstances, but she didn't want her son to be the one to miss out. Somehow, probably with help from my grandparents, she made it happen. We started preparing for the trip weeks in advance because I'd need a passport for the excursion the team would take across the border into Mexico. For most of us, it would be our first time out of the country.

To apply for my passport, we had to send in my birth certificate, and one day, while I was having lunch, I found it on the kitchen table. It was the first time I'd held the official paper in my hands and read it for myself, and what I saw left me confused. My name on my passport wasn't Benjamin Troy Raymond. It was David Antwone Brumfield. Before that moment, I'd only thought of myself as Ben.

I stopped eating and called out to my mother, "Mom! What is this?"

My mother came into the kitchen and sat at the table next to me. "What are you talking about? That's your birth certificate."

"I know," I said, "but the name is different."

"I told you that, Ben," my mother said. "I changed it when you were a baby. Well, we legally changed it when you were five, but we'd already called you Ben for years."

"But how can you just change a kid's name?"

My mother shrugged. "It's not that big of a deal. I wanted a good, strong name for you. We even called you Sonny for a while, but I've always liked Benjamin, and I wanted something from the Bible. I went to court and asked the judge to change it."

"You and my dad went?"

"Just me. But I told him about it later."

She was right. She had mentioned it to me before, but it hadn't clicked in my mind. To see my first-given name crossed off on my birth certificate and replaced by a new name, what I thought of as my real name, completely shocked me. To her it was no big deal—she'd called me Ben for most of my life—but to me it was like discovering I'd been living under a false identity.

It was one more way I was different from the other kids, and I couldn't help wondering what they'd think if they knew. Even though no one could ever find out unless I told them, the name change embarrassed me. I hid my feelings from my mother because I never wanted to upset her, but that revelation lit a small ember of anger in me that would smolder for a long time.

As I grew older, I would come to understand that my original name, David, and the name I was destined to have, Benjamin, both had incredible significance for my life. David, whose name meant "beloved," was a great king in Biblical history. He defied the odds slay the giant, Goliath, even when his own people doubted him. The biblical Benjamin also had his name changed as a young child. His mother, who died in childbirth, had named him Benoni, "son of sorrow." However, his father, Jacob, changed his name to Benjamin, "son of the right hand." I would have to mature over many years to fully comprehend how those two names reflected my place in the world. In the meantime, I was upset and confused.

We went on the trip with the team, and I tried to forget about my birth certificate, and have fun like everyone else. We got to see the Phoenix Suns play. If they were real, then there was a chance that I could one day do what they did and live how they lived. It was the kind of trip so many boys my age would have loved to take, and I was one of the few who got the opportunity. I was a poor kid, being raised by a single mom who struggled to make ends meet, but this was just the first of many trips I'd take around the country. As I played for better and more competitive teams over the coming years, I'd travel all over the country, and I'd do everything I could to see a pro game in every city.

I would even return to Arizona a few years later. Thanks to a turn of good luck with a ticket scalper, we'd land court-side seats on that trip, and in a moment I'd never forget, I'd make eye contact with superstar power forward Charles Barkley. To see the game in person and be acknowledged, even if only for a few seconds, by Sir Charles would make those players I looked up to seem a little more like real people to me. If they could achieve this kind of greatness, I thought, maybe I could too.

But this was my first big trip, and everything was new to me. The desert in Arizona looked like what I'd seen in cartoons, lone cactuses springing up in vast, open spaces. My great-aunt Vera lived out there, and my mother and I had a chance to visit her between activities. Finally, we did cross into Mexico, where barefoot children with snotty noses and dirty hands ran up to us to sell us packs of gum and cheap toys, giving me a whole new perspective on what it really meant to be poor. I bought a sombrero and a poncho and rode on a donkey, typical tourist stuff but brand new experiences for my friends and me.

It was a once-in-a-lifetime adventure for a nine-year-old kid, but through it all, I couldn't stop thinking about that birth certificate. Yes, I was Benjamin Troy Raymond, but I had also been David. I had once shared my father's name, but now there was nothing of that left. My mother and I had the same last name, but I looked so different from her and from the rest of her family. My father's name had been taken from me, and I couldn't remember him well enough to know if we shared the same physical traits or not. I couldn't recall if we looked alike at all or if I was some weird hybrid who came out looking nothing like either of my parents.

So who was I really? It was a question that would take me years of inner struggle and digging deep into family secrets to answer.

CHAPTER SIX

Excuses kill dreams.

One part of my identity I never was questioned was my place as an athlete. From the early success I experienced in second and third grade, every moment on the field or the court felt natural. If I didn't fit in with the way my classmates looked, I also didn't fit in when it came to sports, but for different reasons. I was well ahead of my teammates in my ability to quickly learn and execute new skills. I couldn't take credit for the gifts God had given me, but I certainly enjoyed the benefits.

One of those benefits my athletic talent afforded me was a closer relationship with my grandfather, a die-hard sports fan. He was already in his sixties, a little overweight, and not in any condition to get outside and shoot hoops or throw the football with me, but he was one of my biggest supporters. When I was in fourth grade, my grandfather came to one of my Pop Warner football games, and before the game started, he flashed a twenty-dollar bill at me. "See this, Ben?" he said. "You get your jersey dirty today, and this is for you."

I made sure I got a tackle in that game. It wasn't just the enticement of the money my grandfather had offered me. I also wanted to make him proud of me. He had been the one constant male figure in my life, and he did what he could to fill some of that empty space Slim had left me with when he disappeared from my life for the second time. I didn't want to ever let my grandfather down. No matter how many games he came to or how much he cheered for me, he could never take the place of my missing father, but he provided a sense of stability. He didn't just write checks to help my mother pay the bills and keep a roof over our heads. He showed up for me when it mattered.

Right before I hit fifth grade, my grandfather's health started to suffer, and later that year, he underwent triple bypass surgery. The surgeon transplanted a vessel from his leg to his heart to allow the blood flow to bypass the blockages in three heart arteries and keep his heart pumping. We all expected my grandfather to recover and go on to live a normal, healthy life for many years to come. Unfortunately, it never happened. The bypass surgery probably guaranteed him a little more longevity, but he was never the same again.

After the procedure, this larger-than-life man who had dropped out of high school to go to work, fought in World War II, earned a living as a carpenter, saved to start his own real estate business and lift his family into the ranks of the middle class, and provided for that family over decades, became a shell of his former self. He struggled to relearn the basic life skills most of us take for granted, simple things like how to feed himself and walk on his own. "If I'd known it was going to be like this," he said many times, "I would've never had the surgery."

It wasn't long before the decision-makers in our family realized my grandfather would need round-the-clock care. Given my mother's profession as a nurse and the fact that her father subsidized our life-style, she was the natural choice.

One day, my mother called me into the living room and sat me down on the couch to break the news that we'd be moving soon. "It's a duplex," she said. "So we can live on one side, and your grandparents will be right next door. That way, we'll be close by if your grandfather needs anything."

It had been years since we'd last moved, but the plan made sense to me. I wasn't particularly attached to the house we lived in, so I didn't see a problem with it. Besides, I still believed my grandfather would recover over time, and it would be nice to live so close to my grandparents for a while.

"And it's a better neighborhood," she said. "And you can still go to Grace Lutheran."

I didn't love everything about Grace Lutheran, but I did love playing sports there.

My mother went on. "There's only one problem. We can't take Lady."

She had given me my dog as a gift, and she knew how much Lady meant to me. Lady was more than a pet, and I wasn't about to give her up. "Why can't we take Lady?" I asked.

"They don't allow dogs over there," she explained. "But we'll find a good home for her."

My mother kept talking, but I stopped listening. Lady was getting older, but she was still mine, and I loved that dog. Every night, I fell asleep with my arms wrapped around her neck. During the night, she'd wriggle out of my grasp, and in the morning, I'd find her sleeping beside my bed.

I thought about the time a few years earlier when my mother and I had gone camping and left Lady in the yard with her food and water nearby. When we returned from our weekend trip, Lady was limping and barely getting around on her own four paws. She refused her food, and she didn't want to play. My mother had said that if Lady didn't get better, we'd have to put her to sleep. Later, the paperboy told us that Lady had jumped the fence and gotten hit by a car, and he'd carried her back to the yard. I spent days worrying that Lady would die, but we had gotten lucky, and she had survived. Now, my mother wanted to me to just abandon her, and I wouldn't do it.

"I'm not giving Lady away," I told my mother.

"We don't have a choice, Ben. I have to take care of my father. We have to move."

"Well, I'm not moving without Lady," I shouted. I stomped off to my room, slammed the door behind me, and flopped down on the bed with Lady next to me.

Minutes later, my mother knocked on my bedroom door and eased it open. "You're right, Ben," she said. "It doesn't make sense. If we can't take Lady, then we just won't go."

Right or wrong, my mother was always ready to take my side. She hated to see me upset, but this was one battle I couldn't win. Her father was dying. Not only did she have the expertise to take care of him, but they also had an entangled relationship. She depended on him financially and, in many ways, emotionally. My grandfather supplemented her meager income and bailed her out when she needed it, making sure she got treatment when she had her breakdowns and taking me in when she was gone. He was the reason we always had a roof over our heads. In the end, the decision was made. We had to move. And Lady, the only one I could count on to be there for me at the end of every day, no matter what, had to go.

Losing Lady crushed me. It stoked the small flame of anger already burning in me. Like many young boys, I kept a lot of the things that bothered me to myself because I didn't know who to talk to or what to say and because I'd learned to "suck it up," or at least look like I was. There was no one I could tell that I felt like I'd lost my best friend. I would have other dogs after Lady, but I wouldn't take care of them the way I'd taken care of Lady, and I wouldn't get attached to them. I didn't want to risk that kind of heartbreak again.

We gave Lady to a big family that lived farther out and had more land for her to run and play on. She was a big dog, and the open space would be good for her, but that didn't make me feel any better about the decision. My mother and I moved into one side of the duplex my grandparents owned, and they moved into the other unit. My mother and grandmother worked together to provide my grandfather the care he needed, and I gave all of my attention to sports, where I could escape the reality of sickness, grief, and instability in my life.

———

I had always been a good student, but school began to take a back seat to athletics. I was traveling to tournaments on the weekends, and because I played for my school and for traveling leagues, I had some kind of practice after school every day, and twice a day during the summer. School had become something I had to do but didn't care much about, a necessary chore. I dreaded the schoolwork that awaited me at the start of a new week. It felt like a waste of time.

One Monday during my sixth grade year at Grace Lutheran, my class had a test I knew I wasn't prepared to take. I'd been on the road with my team for most of the weekend, and by the time I got home on Sunday evening, all I wanted to do was lie on the couch and watch a little television until I fell asleep. As I sat at my desk looking at the blank test paper, I really wished I'd cracked a book to prepare, even if only for a few minutes. It was too late to study, but I didn't want to fail.

Rather than accept that I hadn't done what I needed to do, take the failing grade I had coming, and do better next time, I decided to look over at my classmate's paper and copy her answers.

Halfway through the test, my teacher, Mr. Koepke, pushed his seat back from his desk. "Let me talk to you in the hallway for minute, Ben," he said as he headed for the classroom door.

At first, I thought he couldn't be talking to me. I was the only Ben in the class, but I just knew I'd been slick with my cheating, resting my head in my hand and covering the side of my face while my eyes darted to my neighbor's test. As I followed my teacher to the hallway, I tried to convince myself that he hadn't caught me cheating. There was just no way. What I didn't understand was that Mr. Koepke had been in this game much longer than I had, and he was way better at it.

Classes were still in session, so my teacher and I had the hallway to ourselves. Even as a tall-for-my-age sixth grader, I was small next to Mr. Koepke. Well over six feet, wearing size seventeen shoes, my teacher was a monster of a man. Even if he'd been my height, I would've had a hard time looking him in the eye at that moment.

"What did you think you were doing in there?" he asked me in a low voice.

I wasn't dumb enough to rat myself out. He hadn't said the word "cheating" yet, so maybe he really didn't know. "What do you mean, Mr. Koepke?" I asked.

The next thing I knew, I felt my feet lift from the floor as Mr. Koepke wrapped one of his hands in the front of my shirt, yanked me up, and slammed my back into the lockers lining the wall behind me.

"You think I'm stupid, Ben?" he asked. "I saw you in there cheating on that test. What makes you think you get to let someone else do all the work while you take the credit?"

"I'm sorry," I said, trying to keep my voice from shaking.

"So you know what you were doing was wrong?"

I nodded.

Mr. Koepke set me back on my own two feet. "Listen," he said, "you're a smart kid. There's no reason you can't do your own work and make good grades."

My face flushed with embarrassment, and I held back the tears that threatened to spill and embarrass me even more. I prayed no one would come down the hall and witness Mr. Koepke chewing me out.

"Don't throw away your education." Mr. Koepke told me. "You're better than that, Ben."

I mumbled a "Yes, sir" and went back to my desk. I felt nauseous as I struggled through the rest of the test. I'd be lucky to earn a passing grade, but I had no one but myself to blame. I was used to getting pats on the back and high-fives from the adults in my life because they could count on me to help my team take home the win. I could take criticism from a coach when I needed to improve my game, but this was different. Getting called out for a failure of character stung way more.

I felt like a disappointment, but if Mr. Koepke had meant to knock some sense into me, he had succeeded. His message stuck with me. Here was a teacher who cared enough about me and believed in me enough that he wouldn't stand by and let me be labeled as a dumb jock, with no future once I hung up my jersey for good. After that day, sports were still a priority for me, but I made room in my schedule to handle my academics.

―――

As I moved through middle school, I was constantly on the lookout for friends who actually liked me for me. It was easy for me to be popular at Grace Lutheran. Everybody loves a winner, and I set a new record in almost every basketball category—points, rebounds, assists, you name it—and I didn't just break the old school records. I shattered them. Even though I was quickly growing bored with track and field, I took home wins in the 200, 400, and high jump on a regular basis too.

I was the school's star athlete. No one else even came close to my contribution to the success of the school's sports teams, and that kind of achievement drew plenty of attention from my peers. Even though I still got the occasional cracks about my hair, my lips, and my general blackness, kids wanted to be friends with me.

Still, I was never sure if they liked Ben the kid with his own hopes and dreams and struggles or just Ben the star whose shine might rub off on them a little bit. Things were somewhat better for me in the Amateur Athletic League though. Most of my teammates were black like me, and a lot of the guys on my teams came from single-parent homes. A lot of them had dads who showed up to bask in their sons' glory on the court but were nowhere to be found when it was time for a parent-teacher meeting or time to pay for a school field trip.

Even though some of the black kids did give me a hard time for not being black enough, it was still a place where I felt like I could be myself. I could hang out with these guys after practice and do little things like go get a haircut together, and I fit right in.

Eventually, I did find the kind of straight-up, no-b.s. friendship I was looking for, but not where I'd expected to find it. Chad Wiechert and I had crossed paths on the soccer field and in Pop Warner football as young boys. Before I really knew him, I had dubbed him Vanilla Ice because he wore his hair in a swooped over style like the early 90s music artist, famous for being one of the first white rappers to make a mark on the hip-hop scene.

Chad and I had played on the same team in Hoops Club, and in seventh grade, we played on the same Eagles football team. In fact, we both went out for quarterback. I was just as good on the football field as I was on the basketball court—maybe even better—and I got quarterback. Chad was a running back, but there were no hard feelings. We quickly developed a friendship that went beyond teammates.

Later, I recalled that Chad had also come with one of our mutual friends to one of my wrestling parties. My mom was really the pushover mom when I was young. She never said no to me if she could help it, so my house was the fun place to hang out. My friends and I would have parties and watch wrestling on TV or rent movies, knowing we could sneak in an adult film or two and my mom would never know. Chad told me he had been excited to come to the party because he knew me as the all-around athlete in our town. But after we became friends, none of that mattered. We were just two kids having fun.

Chad turned out to be one of the most genuine people I would ever have in my life. He lived in a tough family situation like I did, so he didn't judge me for the ways my family was different. Even though he would always be a die-hard fan, cheering for me even when he wasn't in the game, Chad would have been my friend if I never played another game. I had no doubt that his friendship was real.

When we were hanging out at his house, he didn't give a damn how many points I'd scored in the last game. He pranked me and tormented me just like he did everybody else, and I gave it right back to him. Of course, we were also constantly competing with each other. Half the time, one of us would end up mad because Chad was that kid who would never quit. He just did not know when to say "when." One day, we were playing some game we'd made up with the football, and Chad got angry because I was winning. That kid was so pissed off he grabbed a can of gasoline and dumped it all over me. I was dripping wet and stinking of gas.

That ended the game, but I went inside his house and laid all over the chairs and wallowed all over the couch. It sounds so ridiculous—okay, and even a little dangerous to be playing with gasoline—but we were just doing the kind of ridiculous stuff boys that age did, and neither one of us ever stayed mad at the other.

Over the years, our friendship would have its ups and downs. There would be times when our lives took such different paths we didn't see or talk to each other much, but the friendship we started as young boys playing football and dreaming of becoming professional athletes one day would last for a lifetime.

———

Just before Thanksgiving of 1992, while I was in seventh grade, my grandfather, Lyle Raymond, contracted pneumonia after sitting in the stands to watch me play in a football game. He passed away shortly thereafter. Even though we all knew his health had worsened, the loss hit me hard. It was the first time I ever had to deal with the death of someone close to me.

I would miss spending time with my grandfather and just knowing he was there for me. Not only had he paid my tuition at Grace Lutheran, he'd always supported my school's sports team, and when he died, he left a donation for the school to get new basketball uniforms. Since players couldn't have the same number two years in a row, I had always alternated between number 22 and number 23. The 23 was, of course, for my favorite player of all time, Michael Jordan. When we received our new uniforms, I was given number 23 again.

Because my grandfather had been the one consistent man who showed up at my games and stayed involved in my life, the faculty and administration at Grace Lutheran were very aware of how much he'd meant to me. To honor his contributions to the school and to show their support for me in my time of grief, the school presented me with a plaque dedicated to him. I can still see the eagle emblazoned over 1 Corinthians 28:20: "The Lord God will be with thee; He will not fail thee, nor forsake thee." At that time, I had no idea how true those words had already been in my life.

The school's gesture meant a lot. I was entering a phase of my life filled with uncertainty. I wouldn't be attending Grace Lutheran high school. My grandfather had put me on track to play for Coach Schade, so I'd be going from the small private school to a much larger public school for the first time. I didn't know where my mother and I would be living or how she would manage financially with her father gone. Even more, I worried about who would help her when she had her next breakdown.

Soon after my grandfather passed away, one of my questions was answered when my mother and I moved to a house in the North side of Oshkosh. I needed to be in the right zone to play for Coach Schade, and the move put us in the right place. I hoped the change would be good for my mother too. The duplex was haunted by memories of her father's slow journey to his death, and it had to be hard for her to wake up there every day.

But my mother's mental health was still incredibly fragile. She had little to no coping skills to deal with the loss of the man who had raised her and who had, on more than one occasion, saved her from herself. In the past, she'd used men and drugs to escape the pain. As it turned out, it wouldn't take long for her to run back to both.

————

My time playing for the Racine Racing Rebels left me with some of my best childhood memories. The strongest players in the AAU were recruited from one team to another, year after year. They would promise you more exposure and the chance to play against tougher competition. I joined Racine the same year my grandfather passed away. These were some of the most talented players in the state and the country, and when I was able to not just keep up with them, but often lead the pack, I really understood how great my gift was.

This was the elite group of players that everyone knew had a real chance of playing at the college level one day. Some of us would make it all the way to the NBA. This was like an all-star team, and the coaches really let each kid's skills shine. I felt more at home than ever out there running, the Greyhound let loose on the court. While I led my Grace Lutheran team to the state championships and was incredibly proud of the leadership role I played, my Racine Running Rebels team took third in the nation in an incredibly competitive league. They were both incredible accomplishments, and my confidence that I'd be more than ready to play in high school grew by leaps and bounds.

We were a powerful team, and we would play together for two years before we got pulled to different teams. I would jump from team to team and perform no matter who my coach was or who my teammates were, and that consistency was what began to get me statewide recognition as a powerhouse basketball player.

While I was throwing myself into sports, my mother was hanging on, doing the best she could to deal with her grief after losing her father. Later, as an adult, I would learn how complicated their relationship had been. My mother had relied on him for financial support, guidance in her mental health treatment, and of course, to make sure I had opportunities available to me. But behind closed doors, he also exerted extreme influence over her life. I was too young to see that he'd used her reliance on him to manipulate and control her. When my mother shared the truth with me many years later, it cracked the image of the model grandfather I'd had in my mind and my heart for most of my life.

Although my mother had a hard time staying on balance in the wake of her father's death, she still came out to support me at games and practices. One day, just few months after she'd lost her father, she ran into a man named Jimmy Shepherd at one of our games. Jimmy was the uncle of my teammate, Markyle Green. He was a six-foot-seven-inch, slick-talking, big-city guy. He honed in on my mother and went in for the easy kill. Yes, she was a beautiful woman, but given that she was at one of her lowest points in her life, I'm sure he also saw a weakness in her that he could exploit.

When my mother went outside for a smoke during the game, Jimmy went outside and smoked with her. They had become friends years earlier, but this time, their relationship quickly became much more involved. Soon Jimmy was at our house as much as his own. As they spent more time together, I noticed my mother's behavior changing for the worse.

One day, my mom found a used needle in our house, and when she asked him about it, he claimed his diabetic friend had come over and left the dirty needle behind. My mother knew it was a lie, but she was too meek and needy to put him out and be done with him. She started smoking more weed to deal with the added stress of being involved with Jimmy.

Jimmy was totally caught up in the drug life. He sold and used crack and whatever he was shooting into his veins, and it didn't take my mom long to dive into harder drugs with him. He would go out and smoke crack and cheat on her, so she decided she would go with him. That way, he couldn't cheat on her, but spending more time with him put her on an unstoppable downward slide back into drugs, depression, and paranoia once again.

As I moved into eighth grade, the situation at home only worsened. Little things around the house started to disappear, and any fool could see Jimmy was stealing things like my VCR to get money for drugs. When I confronted my mother about it, she agreed to talk to Jimmy—for all the good it did. Jimmy pointed out how spoiled I was and told her to stop babying me, and nothing changed. He was trying to turn her against me, and she couldn't even see it.

More and more often, my mother came home beaten and bruised after she went away with Jimmy for a day or two. He never hit her in front of me, but it was obvious that he was beating her. My mother covered for him with lies, but she wasn't fooling anyone, not even herself. I had never felt so angry or so helpless.

Since there was no one around to create structure in my life, I didn't have a curfew, and I spent as much time outside of the house as possible. I was either at the park behind our house, over at the high school seeing what kind of game I could get going, or at Chad's house, where he lived with his single mom.

One day, Chad and I were late showing up for the team photo. It was probably because of something I wanted to do to make us stand out in the picture, but my mother immediately blamed Chad. He was developing a reputation as a rebel and a badass, which would only get worse as we entered high school the following school year. But this time, it wasn't his fault.

My mother always believed anything I did wrong was because of someone else's bad influence. This time, she pointed the finger at Chad, and she went off. "I don't want you hanging around him anymore," she finally said. "He's trouble."

For a while, my mother's outburst cost me my best friend. Even at his worst, Chad was never a bad guy, and he would never have done anything to get me in trouble. It was such a minor incident, blown completely out of proportion, and I knew my mother's mental illness and drug abuse were affecting her judgment again, but Chad had no clue.

He'd heard the same rumors everyone else around town had heard, but he had no idea how bad things really were with my mother. My mother's words hurt Chad. He looked at me like a brother, and it was unthinkable to him that he would ever do anything to get me into trouble. My mother wanted him to disappear from my life, and he did.

Living with my mother was like living in a bad made-for-TV movie. She was the addict, the sufferer of mental illness, and the victim of domestic violence. She and Jimmy were running scams to get money for more drugs. She was disappearing with him more and more, sometimes leaving me home alone overnight. I never knew when she'd be home or what kind of shape she'd be in. I had tried talking with her and arguing with her, but nothing changed.

Watching my mother give up and turn her life over to drugs made me sick. I loved her more than anyone on earth, but I had to take control of my own life. I never wanted to be forced into a position to have to make adult decisions at such a young age, but there was no competent adult around to make those decisions for me. I had no choice. It might break my mother's heart and mine, but I had to leave her for my own sake and for hers.

CHAPTER SEVEN

There are no limits, except in your own mind.

The conversation between the two mothers sitting across from each other in the Schades' living room had started off civilly enough, but it hadn't taken long for it to go bad. "He belongs with me!" my mother shouted at Mrs. Schade.

Mrs. Schade kept her voice low. "I know that. We're not trying to take your son from you, Nancy. We just want to help you do what's best for Ben."

"You don't need custody of my son to take care of him," my mother argued.

Sitting on the floor between them, the Schades' German shepherd, Oz, looked back and forth from one woman to the other.

"We're not trying to get custody of your son," said Mrs. Schade. "Guardianship is different. Nobody's taking away your rights as his mother."

As my time living with their family had gone on, Mr. and Mrs. Schade had realized there was no specific timeline for me to go back to living with my mother. In light of that fact, the Schades decided it would be in my best interest for them to become my legal guardians. As it stood, they couldn't even take me to the doctor if I got sick or injured. They couldn't make any decisions for me at school. When it came right down to it, they were hamstrung.

"I'm not losing my son again," my mother shouted. "You're not his mother. I am!" From the moment she'd heard the word *guardianship*, my mother's thoughts had been stuck back in 1980, when I was a ward of the state and my foster mother was the gatekeeper between my real mother and her son. My first foster parents, the Millers, had expressed their desire to adopt me, but my mother had fought hard to keep me. Thirteen years later, she felt like she had to fight again.

"You need to lower your voice," Mrs. Schade told her.

But my mother was past the point of listening to anything Mrs. Schade had to say. Instead, she became more and more upset and defensive. Things escalated until the police were called to restore order, and my mother left without me.

———

When I moved in with the Schades, my mother escaped her volatile relationship with Jimmy and checked in to a rehab center in Chicago. She'd had horrible experiences when she went in for treatment in the 1970s, and she was still terrified of the hospital, but it was what she needed at the time. I traveled to Chicago to visit her, but with schools and sports, I couldn't go often. I felt desperate for her to get better and come home, but weeks and months went by, and she was still in the hospital.

Even though I wasn't waiting up for her at night anymore, worry about my mother's safety and well-being consumed me. Night after night, I sat in my basement room and talked to her on the phone. Sometimes, she was so distraught that I couldn't calm her down. I tried to make the best of it, but I hated hearing the suffering in her voice.

People in our community knew my mother was in treatment, but no one said anything to me about it. Maybe they didn't want to embarrass or upset me, or maybe they just didn't know what to say. Whatever the case, no one brought it up to me, and I didn't try to talk to anyone about it. I had developed a habit of protecting my mother and myself by avoiding conversations about my family life, and that practice continued.

The Schades provided me with a good home. Coach Schade was a hard worker, a disciplined man, and an exceptional basketball coach. He constantly tested my skills and challenged me to be better, never letting me coast on my latest success. Mrs. Schade was a loving mother to their children, Jordan, who we called "Spud," Nikki, and Luke, but she was no pushover. She was a bulldog when it came to her family and running her household. While I lived with them, they both did their best to provide me with their love, their compassion, and their guidance. From the outside, my move to the Schades' home appeared to be a perfect solution. The only problem was that I needed something more.

I had no idea how to articulate what I was missing. Yes, I had a roof over my head and hot, home-cooked meals to eat. Yes, two adults of solid character had generously volunteered to give me a home and take responsibility for me when they absolutely didn't have to do it. Yes, they had given me the support I needed to remove myself from a dangerous situation. And yes, they treated me well, but it was never enough.

I'd never had discipline, structure, and expectations in my home. While the Schades treated me as a welcomed guest, I didn't want to be a guest in anyone's home. I wanted to be a kid, living in a family, with everything that came with having a normal mother and a present father. I craved the kind of attention other kids resented. The bottom line was that I wanted parents. But how could I ask for that?

Looking back, I can see that the Schades were in a tough position and did their best to tread carefully with my mother. They didn't want to box her out or look like they were replacing her. They weren't trying to steal me from her or become my new parents, but the trauma of losing me to foster care when I was an infant had never left my mother, and when word reached her of their plan to become my guardians, her claws came out. It didn't help that Mrs. Schade had known my mother when Nancy Raymond was the "it girl" at their high school. It hurt my mother's pride to have to rely on someone who had once looked up to her.

After my mother was discharged from rehab, she phoned Mr. and Mrs. Schade more and more often, and when she did, she was antagonistic and accusatory. She swore she would never let them become my guardians. Her constant calls and unexpected visits disrupted the family's peaceful daily routine. No matter how much Mrs. Schade tried to reassure her, my mother was convinced the Schades were her enemies.

———

My mother was relentless in her mission to put some distance between the Schades and me. Although she was just getting back on her feet and was in no position to care for me herself, no one could convince her that I was fine right where I was. The tug-of-war she created with the Schades had become a battle she would win or die trying. Finally, the Schades decided it would be better for everyone, including me, if I left their home.

I was so broken and defeated. When they gave me the news, I felt like I was being rejected from every direction. A part of me believed the Schades should have done more to keep me there with them. A part of me resented my mother for messing things up so that I had to move again. I'd just gotten used to the way the Schades' household ran, and now it was time to go and learn the personalities and routines of another family. Maybe I wouldn't fit in there. Maybe they wouldn't want me to stay. Maybe they would reject me too.

As I packed my things, I hid my sadness, fear, and hurt behind a wall of anger. If I had to go, then fine. I'd go, and no one would know how I really felt about it. As I headed to the front door, Mrs. Schade held out her arms to me. "Can I have a hug, Ben?" she asked.

I walked right past her.

I appreciated what they'd done for me. I really did. But I couldn't escape my fear that they loved Ben, the basketball player who led the team. I wasn't convinced that they loved Ben, the teenage boy, for nothing more than being myself. My mixed feelings would last for years. Even in college, I would resent Coach Schade for not coming to any of my games after all I had done for his high school basketball program. While I played for him, he had taken our team to see one of his former students play at Vanderbilt University, so I couldn't understand why he wouldn't come out and support me.

I convinced myself that I had never mattered to the Schades, and the thought hurt me. When their son got married, I still wasn't ready to reconcile my feelings for the family. I didn't go to his wedding, even though I could have made it. I still hadn't shaken that bitterness, but I eventually would.

More than a decade after they first took me in, after I had the benefit of more life experience, some healing, and some distance from my childhood wounds, I would return to Oshkosh to visit the Schades, and I would apologize. I should have focused much more on appreciating what they had given me and much less on what I'd failed to find in their home. They were a good family who reached out to me when I needed it most, and it was important to me that they know I regretted the way I'd behaved. Thankfully, they understood.

———

The soundtrack of my freshman year consisted almost exclusively of hip hop music. Warren G and Nate Dog's "Regulate" was a favorite I played so much I can't think of that time period without hearing the lyrics in my head. That same year, 1994, Shaquille O'Neal came out with "Biological Didn't Bother." It was the first song released on his second album, and even though it barely broke into the *Billboard* Hot 100, it struck home for me. In the song, Shaq celebrates his stepfather for stepping in to help Shaq's single mother raise her son after his biological father abandoned him. The song makes it clear that Shaq wants nothing to do with the man who brought him into the world, and as I rapped along with my CD, I felt the same way.

"Biological Didn't Bother" tapped into that deep well of anger in me. Not only did I feel the same way about Slim—if he didn't want me when I was a child, he'd better not come around once I'd made it—I also resented that there'd been no one to step in and fill the shoes Slim had left empty. Of course, I knew I wasn't the only teenage boy growing up without a dad or a stepdad to guide him to manhood, but the song put into words a lot of what I rarely expressed.

Because my mother still wasn't in a position to create a home for me, I moved in with Tom Nesbitt, my freshman football coach, his wife, Gloria, and their sons, Mike and Tim. They were a loving, easygoing family, and I was relieved to find I fit in well there. Chad came over a lot, and he, Mike, and I spent most of our time outside playing football games. During that time, the three of us became close friends.

Things turned out to be much less tense between the Nesbitts and my mother, so home life was much less stressful for me. Mr. and Mrs. Nesbitt were aware of all of the conflicts between my mother and the Schades, and they were careful not to do anything that might give her even the slightest hint that they were replacing her in my life. It also helped that my mother didn't have the kind of history with their family that she had with the Schades. They didn't see her as someone who'd once had it all but had lost it. For the most part, the Nesbitts only knew her as she was.

Just like the Schades were a basketball family, the Nesbitts were a football family. A love of the game was something we all shared in common. I'd been a fan of the Packers since I was old enough to hold a football, and when the Nesbitts took me to see Brett Favre and my favorite team play, I couldn't have been more excited. It was one of the best days I'd had in a long time. My time with the family really was a lot of fun.

I spent my freshman year packing my bag and bouncing from one home to another. The Schades and the Nesbitts all tried to do their very best for me, but I never stopped wondering if I'd ever really be a part of a family. I never stopped dreaming of a place where my ability as an athlete wouldn't play a role in whether or not I belonged there.

The upheaval I started high school with turned out to have one benefit. Without my mother around to protest, Chad and I had renewed our friendship. When my mother found out we were hanging out again, she wasn't happy, but by then, I'd figured out that I could choose my own friends and there wasn't much she could do about it.

Chad and I were on the freshman football team together, and ninth grade would turn out to be a standout year for me. I was one of the first freshmen to play on the varsity basketball team, but as starting quarterback, I'd also lead the freshman football team to its first undefeated season. I felt like I was taking high school athletics by storm, but the year held a downturn for Chad.

He had always been a badass on the field, but that year, Chad had a moment that changed the way he saw the game. He was a hard hitter, but he had a dangerous habit of tackling with his head down. Coaches were constantly warning him that he was going to get hurt, and eventually, he did. Chad went in for a tackle, once again with his head down, and almost as soon as he made contact, he crumpled to the ground.

It was scary to see my closest friend lying on the field, unable to get up and walk on his own. It must have been even scarier for him, looking up at the sky and wondering how bad his neck injury really was. Medics carried Chad off the field on a stretcher, and after that day, the game was never the same for him.

The next year, we would play on the junior varsity football team together, and I'd suit up to punt and play free safety for the varsity team, but Chad was done. At some point during our sophomore year, he would quit football. It would also be my last year playing. Once I started to feel like players were going after my knees, I'd let football go and focus on basketball instead.

We had been teammates since seventh grade, but our friendship went beyond sports and lasted after Chad gave up sports altogether. We found time to hang out whenever we could, and it was always an adventure. Some of those adventures were a little more risky than others, but they were always good for a story.

One day, we left school to go to lunch. Chad was driving, and before he pulled into the street looked both ways. He really did, but on the left side, a baseball field blocked the view. He really needed to inch up and look that way again to see what was coming, but he was ready to go.

Chad floored it and darted into the street. And ran square into the side of a city bus. His Mercury Cougar bounced off the bus and spun out in the street in front of the school. When the car game to a stop, we looked at each other in disbelief. Then we scrambled out of the car. We were lucky to be alive, but the fact that we came out of it unharmed also gave everyone license to give Chad hell about it. I couldn't count the number of times someone asked him, "How can you not see a city bus? It's a bus!"

————

By the time I hit tenth grade, my mother was mentally and emotionally up to living on her own and managing a home for us again, and I left the Nesbitts to live with her. Even though I was a little worried that it wouldn't last, my hopes were high for her to stay on track this time. She had completed her treatment program, we had a support system in my assistant coach, who lived three doors down from our apartment and had really taken me under his wing, and the Nesbitts and Schades were still keeping an eye out for me. My athletic achievements had earned me a certain amount of hometown fame, and a lot of people tried to make sure I didn't have to do without. In doing so, they also looked out for my mother.

My mother had never enjoyed much financial stability. When she was able to hold a job, it was often part-time or temporary work, and the jobs were typically the kinds of home health care positions that didn't pay much. Things were no better this time around, but somehow, we always made ends meet. When my mother came to me and said, "I don't think we're going to make the rent this month," it still got paid. Although I didn't know it at the time, those were months when members of our community stepped in and made sure my mother and I could make it through one more month living together.

I was cautiously happy, but my life was busier than ever. I was still playing travel basketball, even though my high school coach was starting to give me a hard time about it. "You're choosing a traveling team over your school," Coach Schade told me. "You're missing tournaments. You're missing important events when you should be here."

I put Coach Schade off, but it was reaching the point when I'd have to make a choice, and in fact, junior year would be my last year playing travel ball. In the meantime, I played for my high school, and I played for the Milwaukee Pal. Through it all, my mother was still a sports mom at heart. She showed up for all of my games, and she didn't go unnoticed by the single men in the stands.

———

One summer day after my sophomore year ended, I heard footsteps in the basement of the duplex where my mother and I lived together. I could tell more than one person was moving around, so I decided to check it out. There sat my mother, talking with a stranger. He was a tall, light-skinned black guy with an athletic build, but the first thing I noticed about him was the ankle monitor on his leg. I figured he was fresh out of prison, and it turned out that I was right.

My mother had met Derrel Wilkerson at one of my Milwaukee Pal basketball games. In the story they tell, they chatted for a while, and when Derrel asked if he could call her some time, she said sure. But when he called the number she gave him, a recording answered, "You've reached the Women's Correctional Institute."

When Derrel saw my mother at the next game, he told her, "You could have just turned me down, you know. You didn't have to be smart about it and give me the wrong number."

My mother laughed and assured him that she hadn't done it on purpose, and this time, she made sure he had the correct number. For many years, I would think it was one of the worst decisions she could have made.

That day in the basement, my mother introduced me to Derrel and told me they'd been getting to know each other for a few months. I greeted him with my arms folded and a look of suspicion. It would have been difficult to get excited about anyone with a recent criminal history who wanted to spend time with my mother. I always wanted to protect her against her own bad judgment, especially when it came to men.

Derrel had recently done two years for some kind of insurance scheme. He was out on work release, and even though he lived in Milwaukee and we lived in Oshkosh, he and my mother went back and forth between the two cities, spending the day together when they could.

Over the course of weeks, Derrel started to grow on me. He had the kind of friendly charm that could win anyone's heart. Friendly and laidback, he was a natural storyteller, and even though we soon discovered most of his stories came with his own unique blend of truth and fiction, in the beginning, he was interesting to listen to and talk sports with. He had been a phenomenal athlete in his younger days, and he was still in decent shape.

I started calling him D-Wilks, and I took him to open gyms to play ball with me. He smoked a pack a day, so he couldn't run the court like he used to, but he could still grab the rim. He was one of the few black men around, and I enjoyed his company. Besides my grandfather, who had never been in any condition to go out and shoot hoops, Derrel was the first man in my mother's life who took that kind of interest in me.

Chad thought Derrel was a lot of fun. My coaches got to know him, and they took to him too. People gravitated to Derrel because he had a friendly, open personality and the natural magnetism of a gifted storyteller who could keep you interested and entertained even when you doubted the truth of his tale. They were the traits of a guy who would be popular wherever he went. They were also the skills that made him a semi-competent con artist.

CHAPTER EIGHT

Discipline closes the gap between where you
are and where you want to be.

Things between my mother and her new boyfriend moved way too fast for my taste, and before I knew it, they announced that they were getting married. In spite of my grudging acceptance of Derrel, I refused to go to the church and witness my mother and him becoming husband and wife. They'd only known each other a year or so, and I couldn't understand why they were in such a rush to get married. "You know you don't need to do that, right? Why do you want to marry this guy?" I asked my mother, but she had made up her mind.

My mother must have been really hurt by my attitude because I got a call from our pastor about it. He encouraged me to do the right thing and show up for my mother's wedding. "You have to do be there for your mom," he told me.

I was torn. Derrel wasn't the man I would have picked for my mother, and I didn't trust that he would all of a sudden walk the straight and narrow just because they got married. As angry and suspicious as I was, my mother really didn't have anyone else in her corner. I did go to the wedding, but I went under protest. As much as I loved looking fly, I voiced my objection to their marriage through my choice of wedding attire. I threw on my Air Force 1 sneakers, shorts, and an old sweater. I thought the happy couple was lucky I showed up at all. I was their sole witness, and I didn't want to be there.

There wasn't one specific moment when I realized Derrel and my mother were headed down a bad road. With Derrel, the signs were harder for me to see in the beginning. For one thing, I didn't know him as well, so I wasn't as clued in to his habits and behaviors. And on the surface, using didn't change Derrel the way it did some people. This was a man who could smoke crack and almost seem like his normal self. He hid it well, and he never used in my presence.

My mother was a different story. When she started using again, it was obvious. Small lies that would seem like innocent mistakes coming out of anyone else's mouth; missing appointments and showing up late for important events; running out of money all the time; mood swings and blowing insignificant things out of proportion; sleeping too much or not enough; disappearing for hours, or even days, without explanation; unprovoked defensiveness; and a sense that she was always hiding something—they were all telltale signs.

Early in their relationship, I'd pulled Derrel aside to talk man to man. "The only things I ask of you," I'd said, "is that you don't hit her and you don't get her back on drugs." In my mind, my mother's drug use was always tied to some man she was seeing. Because of her mental illness, and because I loved her, I let her off the hook somewhat. I had to point the finger at someone. I wanted to blame someone else for her poor choices, just like she always blamed one of my friends when I got into any trouble. They both bore responsibility, but my allegiance was to my mother, and all I could see was that she was headed for self-destruction again.

When money I'd saved was missing from my dresser drawer, Derrel was quick to say one of my friends must have stolen it, but I knew what was up. Slowly at first, and then faster, anything of value was disappearing from our home. Within a few of months, Derrel and my mother were on a tear. They were running minor check-cashing schemes and borrowing money from anybody willing to part with a dollar, often under the guise of needing to buy something for me.

It was the same old song. My mother even pleaded with my girlfriend's parents for money. I had warned my girlfriend that it could happen and made her promise to tell me if either my mother or Derrel came around asking for money. "They'll give you a sob story, but don't fall for it," I'd told her. "Tell your parents not to give them anything no matter what they say."

I had specifically asked my mother to stay away from my girlfriend's family. "You're going to ruin this relationship for me if you drag them into your mess," I'd warned. But the need for money, ultimately a need to buy drugs, outweighed the cost of my humiliation.

———

Living with two adults caught up in their addiction made me feel like I could never turn my back for a minute. I couldn't trust anything Derrel said, and my mother walked a line between trying not to upset me and backing up his lies.

Just when I thought they'd run out of things to rip from our home and sell for cash, my most prized possessions disappeared.

"What happened to my cards? Where are they? I'm sick of this!" I yelled.

I stood in front of the closet in the middle of our duplex. Mostly, it was filled with boxes and the kind of junk you save just in case you need it, but which you never actually go back to use. It was rare that anyone went in that closet for anything. That was why I'd hidden my collectible trading cards in there. I'd buried them down deep in a back corner, but I'd underestimated the addict's resourcefulness.

My mother stepped into the hallway to see what had me so upset. "It was probably one of your friends," she explained.

The moment I'd slid my hand behind a stack of boxes and reached for the cherry-red box I kept my cards in, my hand had found empty space, and I'd known. The cards I'd spent years collecting, trading, and carefully storing and protecting were gone. I'd started collecting sports cards when I was just a little boy and neighborhood police had handed them out to us kids. Over the years, I'd added several valuable cards to my collection. That box contained rookie cards for all the greats in the NFL and the NBA, including Jerry Rice, Michael Jordan, Charles Barkley, Karl Malone, Shaquille O'Neal, and so many others.

Derrel came in and stood next to my mother, and she told him, "Ben's cards are missing."

"That's funny," Derrel said, "I'm missing a pair of my dress shoes too. Somebody must have been in here."

I lost it. I punched my fist right through the hallway wall and screamed at him, "Nobody stole your busted-ass shoes! You think I'm stupid?"

Talking over each other, the two of them launched into a story, trying to convince me they had nothing to do with my missing cards, but I didn't want to hear any more lies. I stormed out of the house and slammed the door behind me before things could get any worse.

They were so caught up in feeding their habit that I was really just an afterthought. Neither of them understood the depth of the betrayal I felt. A theft is always a violation, but when someone who's supposed to care about you is willing to steal what you prize most, it's like a slap in the face. Derrel might have been behind the whole thing, but he and my mother were in this together. They'd sold a card collection worth several thousand dollars, and more importantly, filled with priceless memories, for fifty bucks worth of crack.

Years later, after I was already grown, my mother would give me a huge collection of cards. She wanted to make up to me for the loss of that day, and her effort touched me. Unfortunately, what was stolen from me on that day couldn't be replaced.

Not long after that incident, I was driving through town when I saw my mother and her husband straggling down the street. My mother had just been released from the hospital after checking in for rehab again, and they obviously weren't a happy couple out for a little exercise. They were walking because they had no other way to get home. It was a sad sight, and I shook my head and stopped to talk to them.

"Hey, Derrel," I said, "you remember what I told you when you first started seeing my mom?" I got out of the car and reminded Derrel of the conversation he and I had early in their relationship. He had never put his hands on her, but he had broken his other promise to me. He had taken her right back to drugs. I was done with him at that point. I cussed him out, and we stood there yelling at each other. There's no winning an argument with an addict who's using. You're fighting with the drug. The man can't even hear you. I had my say and climbed back in my car.

Derrel yelled at me, "You're not even gonna give your mom a ride?"

I did give her a ride, but I told her, "He's not getting in this car." With my mother in the passenger seat, I peeled out and left Derrel to walk the rest of the way.

As we drove home, I tried to talk some sense into my mother, but I saw the writing on the wall. Things were going to get worse before they got better. Derrel and my mother were going to have to bottom out before they made a change.

———

While my junior year found my family falling apart, I still had basketball, and 1996 turned out to be my best year yet as an athlete. I was captain of the team, averaging over twenty points per game. After almost every game, articles in the local papers reported my accomplishments on the court. That year, I went all-conference and all-state, confirming my status as one of the best basketball players in the state of Wisconsin.

When we met our rivals on our own turf for a huge game, the crowd packed the stands. Chad was there, leading the cheers and hyping up the crowd. As usual, my mother was there too, and Derrel joined her to watch me play. Fond du Lac had a serious basketball pedigree, and either their team or ours would represent our region in the state tournament. As we neared the end of the game, the score was so close that it could go either way.

Our team was down one. The entire crowd knew where the ball was going, and they were cheering for Raymond to bring home the win. The opposing team knew it too, and all eyes were on me.

It was the kind of moment I lived for. I blocked out the noise of the crowd and the voices of my teammates. The seconds seemed to crawl by as all those days of shooting the last-second shot in practice and in open gyms came back to me. All those times when I'd envisioned hitting the shot when it mattered most, all those times when I'd gone there in my mind and made it happen, had finally become reality.

As soon as the ball hit my hands, I dribbled towards the free-throw line. Sweat dripping off my forehead, I pulled up as high as I could. As I released the ball and followed through, I heard the crowd gasp with anticipation—and I nailed the game-winning shot at the buzzer.

We won!

The crowd's gasp turned into whoops and shouts of joy. Before I could start to celebrate, the fans were on me, mobbing me, screaming my name, crushing me. It was the best feeling in the world—just as I'd imagined it would be. I felt like a hero, like I had done something significant, not just for myself and my team but for our school and our town. Hearing the crowd go wild with excitement and jubilation and knowing I was responsible for all that joy was an awesome experience. At the same time, when you're mobbed like that, it's almost like being trampled. Arms wrapped around my throat as people hugged their congratulations. It was all I could do to scream, "Get off me! I can't breathe!" I fought my way to open air, but I loved every minute of it. Every extra minute, when I'd stayed late or shown up early to practice just a little more, had been worth it.

In my eyes, the only stain on that perfect moment was Derrel's presence. He wanted to celebrate my win just like everyone else, but I was so angry with him about the way he and my mother were living that I didn't want anything to do with him. I brushed him off.

With a few more wins, it was official. Our team was going to the state tournament. Leading up to the game, I couldn't go anywhere at school or in the city without someone coming up to me to talk about the tournament. It was a big deal for everyone, and it was the kind of attention I thrived on. The school held a pep rally for the team, and I thanked everyone for supporting us and cheering us on. It meant a lot to me to have so many people behind us.

It was the kind of experience that every athlete dreams of having. Everyone wants to play in the championship. That's why you practice day after day, standing there with sweat dripping off of you, getting in a few more free throws after everyone else has gone home. It's why, even when you feel like you could fall to the floor, you push yourself through those final wind sprints. It's why you sacrifice other school activities most students get to enjoy in their free time. It's all for that moment, for that chance to showcase your talents and skills.

The day of the game, I felt good. Everything had been leading up to that moment. Watching our competition warm up, some of my teammates got nervous. They were feeling intimidated, but I pumped them up, reminding them that we had earned our spot in that tournament and we had just as much of a chance to win as the other team did.

It seemed like our entire student body had come to see us play. My grandmother, Aunt Bonnie and her husband, Jack, and my cousins were all there in the stands with my mother and Derrel. As the announcer called our names, one by one, my teammates and I jogged into the stadium to thunderous cheers and deafening applause. All eyes were on us. All eyes were on me.

Out in the stands the fans waved hand-painted signs in the air. "Raymond Leads Us!"

"You can't catch the Greyhound!"

"Go B-Ray!!!"

They were cheering for me, number twenty-three.

That year, no one else on my travel team had made it that far with their high school team. I was really proud to have led my team so far. Playing basketball on that level, putting my skills to the test against the top high schools in our state, was the best feeling during one of the worst times. I was on top of the world.

My junior year was ending, and I was wrapping it up with complete confidence that I'd receive college scholarship offers. I felt good, and when I found myself dominating a player I'd always looked up to in a pick-up game, my confidence only grew. Frank Seckar had played for Coach Schade when I was only a ball boy for the team. In fact, he was the player Coach Schade had taken us to watch play at Vanderbilt. Frank had been great in high school, and he was a star on his college team. I had grown into my skills enough to match this player I'd admired for so long.

Frank swept the ball from left to right to dribble past me, and as I reached in, my hand tangled in his jersey. I heard a pop, and pain surged through my right hand—my shooting hand.

Clutching my hand to my chest, I headed for the locker room, screaming, "Sh—!" at the top of my lungs. Behind me, I heard my friends laughing. They knew me as a jokester, and they figured I was trying to prank them again.

There was no question in my mind. Something was seriously wrong with my hand. The knuckle of my middle finger was pushed down and the bone stuck up at an unnatural angle. I couldn't believe this was happening just before my last year of high school. Images of a year without basketball, no college offers, and no way to get out of Oshkosh flashed through my mind, and I punched a locker door with my good hand.

Driving with my left hand, I made my way to the emergency room and called my mother to meet me there. When a nurse came in after I'd had x-rays, I asked her for the truth. "Just tell me," I said. "Is it broken?"

She frowned and shook her head. "You'll have to wait for Dr. Finger," she told me.

My mother and I looked at each other and cracked up. Dr. Finger was going to treat my broken finger. It was the most ridiculous thing, and even with the pain and the worry, the two of us couldn't stop laughing.

As it turned out, my hand was actually broken. I left the hospital with a cast up to my elbow. I'd been looking forward to a summer of basketball and an amazing senior year, but it wouldn't be so easy. I went to work training myself to shoot with my left hand, but my right arm got weaker and weaker from lack of use. When the doctor x-rayed my hand and found out that the bone wasn't healing, I knew I was in trouble. If I had to wear that cast much longer, the muscles of the arm would completely atrophy.

Luckily, one of the athletic staff at my high school used his connections to get me in to see Dr. Patrick McKenzie. Dr. McKenzie was the team physician for the Green Bay Packers and an expert in caring for sports injuries. He got me out of that full cast and put me in a brace that kept the broken bone stable while allowing me to use the hand. I was back in action—sort of.

After a few weeks later, I was itching to get back on the court. I stood a foot away from the basket and shot with my right hand. I watched as the ball went up and then dropped like a rock right at my feet. I had a long way to go to rebuild my strength and relearn how to shoot, but I didn't quit. I went into physical therapy and practiced whenever I could. By summer, I wasn't at one hundred percent yet, but I was getting there, and I played fairly well in the AAU tournament with the Milwaukee Pal.

Earning a scholarship and getting a college degree became even more important to me as my hand healed. A career-ending injury could happen to any athlete at any time. More than ever, I realized that included me.

―――――

My injury improved, but thing at home only got worse. It didn't take long for the downfall I'd predicted for my mother and Derrel to come true. By the end of my junior year, all of their scheming had caught up to them. They went into a grocery store and cashed a stolen check, and minutes later, the police stopped them and arrested them both.

They each faced criminal charges, but she was a pretty white woman with mental illness and no criminal history. He was a black man still on parole. Charges against my mother were dropped and her record wiped clean on the condition that she get treatment again, serve two years' probation, and pay restitution. D-Wilks was sentenced to twenty-five months in the Milwaukee-Oak Hill correctional center for writing bad checks and for violating his parole. He not only had to serve time for this new offense, the twenty-five months included time he'd avoided serving from a previous sentence when he'd been paroled. My mother would visit him there to celebrate their first wedding anniversary.

My mother went into the hospital, and after staying alone in the apartment for a while, I finally moved back in with the Schades to finish the school year. When she came out of treatment, once again, my mother was broke and unemployed. Of course, the apartment was long since lost too. She moved into a rundown, pay-by-the week motel and stayed there for as long as she could. Finally, she turned to her family for help again.

It seemed like my high school years would end the same way they had begun, with instability, insecurity, and that same sense of loneliness that had haunted me for so much of my life. I was sure that I'd spend my senior year struggling to find a place to call home and still wishing for that elusive sense of family. But God works in mysterious ways, and I couldn't have been more wrong about what my future held.

CHAPTER NINE

Practice does not make perfect. Only perfect practice makes perfect. —Vince Lombardi

During the summer before my senior year, I went through that common teenage rite of passage of having my wisdom teeth pulled. All four of mine were impacted to the bone, and the dentist told me I would have to go under general anesthesia, and I'd need a couple of days to recover. With Derrel in jail and my mother back living in Beaver Dam, Aunt Bonnie and her family took me in, but where I would go after that, I didn't know. I had just come off the high of an amazing junior year as an all-state athlete and having led my team to the state tournament, but since Beaver Dam was out of my school district and too far to commute every day, I couldn't live there.

After I was back on my feet, my mother and Aunt Bonnie took me to a duplex in Beaver Dam. "This is where we're going to be living now," my mother said.

Aunt Bonnie said, "There's a good school nearby, Wayland Academy. You can go there, and you'll be able to keep your basketball skills up and get ready for college."

It was my senior year. I was looking forward to my last season playing basketball with my team at Oshkosh North and to all the things seniors did—homecoming, prom, senior prank and parties, and graduating with the classmates I'd spent the last three years with. Now, my family wanted me to give up all of that. "No, I'm not doing it. I'm not moving out here," I told them.

I had been bounced around my entire life. I understood that my mother needed to be close to her support system, but that didn't mean I had to lose everything I cared about in my own life.

They tried to explain to me why this was the best thing for all of us, and I started going off. Aunt Bonnie slipped away to give my mother and me time to talk it out. She probably thought my mother would calm me down and convince me that this was the best decision for everyone, but I wasn't budging.

With my mother, I was completely honest. "What more do you guys want to take from me? I've been moved everywhere," I said, "and I've never done anything wrong to deserve it. I do my schoolwork, I stay out of trouble, and I play basketball. That's it. I've never given you any problems, but I'm telling you that if you guys try to make me move and go to this Wayland Academy, I will quit basketball and drop out of school."

In a healthy family, those words might have come across as the melodramatic ranting of a disgruntled teenager, but I meant every word of what I said. If I had to turn my life upside down again, then I wasn't going to be bothered with any of it anymore. My mother must have known I was serious because she gave up trying to convince me to follow their plan.

A couple of days later, I went back to my high school to register for my senior year classes, but I was completely dejected. I was at another crossroads. I couldn't go down the road my mother and Aunt Bonnie wanted me to go down, but I had no idea how I'd follow my own path. I couldn't go to school there unless I found somewhere to live before the new term started.

Not long after that, I went to a party at Evan Hughes's house. I knew Evan from sports, but we weren't particularly close at the time. For some reason, he was thinking about my situation, and that night he let his mom know I had nowhere to go.

Before the party was over, Mrs. Hughes pulled me aside. "You can stay here for a few days while you figure things out, Ben."

It was a kind offer, especially since I was just one of a bunch of kids in their house that night and she didn't really know me. Mrs. Hughes didn't press me for details about my predicament, which was good. At the time, I was filled with such a mix of emotions, I might have said anything.

With no clue about how long their hospitality would last, I stayed with the Hughes family for a few days. Mrs. Hughes had a little office off the kitchen, and she was a night owl, staying up until three or three thirty in the morning most nights. When the house was quiet late at night, I'd go in and talk to her. I'd recline in a chair, and she'd work at her computer, and we'd talk for hours about whatever was on our minds. It quickly became our nightly ritual.

The days turned into weeks, and eventually, Mr. and Mrs. Hughes told me that if I didn't have anywhere else to stay, I could stay with them for my senior year. It was a perfect solution for me since Evan and I went to the same high school, but I had to get my mother's agreement, and that meant convincing my aunt first.

I wrote my aunt a note pleading with her to let me stay with the Hughes family. All summer she'd been pushing for me to move out to Beaver Dam because, as far as she could see, I had nowhere else to go. Now I had a new and better option. "If you let me do this," I wrote, "I'm going to be the most determined student you've ever seen. I signed the letter and sent it to my aunt, but it was really a contract with myself. I committed to being focused in my schoolwork and in my personal life to make the most of the opportunity Mr. and Mrs. Hughes were giving me. In my mind, the decision was already made. I was staying with the Hugheses.

———

The Hughes family's home was one of the biggest houses I'd ever been in at that time. Compared to the places where I'd grown up, it felt like a sprawling mansion, and because it was white, I started calling it the White House. Between the big home and the family-owned business, I assumed the family was very well off.

Soon after I got there, Evan challenged me to dunk on his rim, and of course, I went for it. I did dunk on him, but I ripped the rim right off. Immediately, I wanted to turn time back a few minutes and blow Evan off. I was sure I was about to get put out of the house, but Evan was happy because he really wanted a new rim. That was why he had me out there dunking in the first place.

Luckily, Evan's parents didn't make a big deal of it. They just went out and got him a new rim. I was relieved. Nobody mentioned kicking me out for destroying their property. The incident also reinforced my impression that the family had money to spare.

What I didn't know, and wouldn't discover for years, was that the Hughes family was in the middle of a financial crisis. An employee had stolen money from their business, and they were doing damage control to get back on stable footing. They were struggling, but they never made that a burden on their children. They had expectations of their sons, but they didn't expect them to take on adult problems.

Allowing me to live in their home had to add to their money stress. I was a big, active kid, and I ate and drank like one. Mom Kat, the name I quickly started calling Mrs. Hughes, would come home with gallons of fruit punch and my favorite Chicken in a Biskit crackers. I would sit in the living room and down a box of the crackers, kill half of the fruit punch, and still be hungry for dinner.

When I first got there, I still had my habit of hiding food in my bedroom. It wasn't that I thought anyone was going to take it from me, but I was used to living with a food shortage at my mother's house. Whenever there was extra, I felt like I needed to hoard it and make it last because there might not be enough next time. I had been in survival mode for a long time, and it would take me some time to get out of it. Eventually, Mom Kat realized what I was doing. She explained that there was always enough food in their house, and I didn't need to store any away for rough times.

Even though I undoubtedly made the household grocery bill multiply, no one complained or told me to stop eating so much. What I realized later was that, even though I had added to the financial strain, the night I went to Evan's party was a moment of divine intervention. The Hughes family was just what I needed, a two-parent household with boys I could hang out with, a loving mother, and a strong father figure, but I was also just what they needed. I quickly became a big brother to the boys, especially young Tommy, but in many ways, I was also the additional son Mom Kat needed in her life at the time. We were all destined to come together when we did, and that more than outweighed the hurting I put on their bank account.

———

Going into my senior year, I had a steady girlfriend, and because we'd been dating for a while and I really liked her, I wanted to do some kind of significant gesture to let her know how I felt. I wasn't even close to thinking about marriage yet, and I wouldn't be for a long time, but I decided to get her a promise ring to show her I cared about her. I saved money from my job and skipped lunches to hold on to my lunch money. It was that important to me to give her that gift.

Somehow, the ring became a subject of debate for my family, and some of my relatives thought I absolutely should not buy the ring for my girlfriend. At the time I couldn't figure out why it was such a big deal, but it was. Finally, I talked to Mom Kat about it. She saw it as a thoughtful gift, and she agreed that the way I was going about paying for it with my own money was a good idea.

When I told my family I was moving forward, Mom Kat stood with me. She said it was my money, so I should be able to spend it on a gift for my girlfriend if that was what I wanted to do. There was some back and forth, but I lived at the Hugheses' house, and no one could really stop me from buying the promise ring.

At that time, I had no idea how much went on between adults outside of the eyes and ears of kids like me. Years later, I found out that Mom Kat paid a price for standing with me on my decision. Unbeknown to me, my family had agreed to give Mr. and Mrs. Hughes a small amount of money every month to help cover the cost of raising me. When Mom Kat didn't go along with their plan to stop me from buying the ring, the money dried up.

From that point on, Hugh and Mom Kat provided for all of my room and board even though they were already financially strapped. They could've easily said they couldn't afford to keep me there anymore, and no one would've blamed them, not even me. Instead, they figured out a way to make it work, and they never let it become my problem. They left me out of adult conflicts and just let me be a kid.

At the same time, being a kid in the Hughes family didn't mean running wild and doing whatever you wanted. Mom Kat ran the household, but Hugh had a set of standards he expected all of us boys to live up to without exception. It was a new way to live for me. Between my mother's guilt about the ways she had failed me, and leaving me alone while she was off doing drugs with the men in her life, she had never set expectations for my behavior. She more or less let me do what I wanted and come and go as I pleased. That wouldn't fly in the Hughes house.

When I had a girl in my room with the door closed, it didn't take Mom Kat long to shut that down. "That's not how we do things here," she told me. "These are the rules." She was always the one to give me that kind of correction, and she did it in a way that was kind and loving but not to be questioned.

One day, Evan and I were leaving for a basketball game and Evan, who was on the j.v. team, was flipping out because he was sure we were going to be late.

"Evan," I said, "I'm the MVP. That bus ain't leaving if they want to win the game."

That was the kind of attitude Hugh had no patience for. He didn't care if I was the MVP. I had to get out of that bed early because that was what men did. The first morning I heard him yell at us, "Get your asses up out of the bed!" I came flying downstairs, sure I was late for class. When I got to the kitchen, I saw that we still had an hour before I had to leave.

Hugh was teaching us that a man doesn't wait to the last minute and rush out the door, hoping he'll only be a little late. He was showing us a real work ethic. The Nesbitts and the Schades had shown me great examples of work ethic too, but Hugh took it a step farther. He didn't just show it to me; he demanded it of me just as he demanded it of his own sons. Given the complete lack of structure I'd grown up with in my mother's house, Hugh's lessons were just what I needed. Even more importantly, they came as I needed them, without sugarcoating.

Later on, when it was clear I would be staying for a while, Hugh told me, "If you're staying here, you need to have job." It was that simple, and you'd better believe, I did go out and find work.

———

From the beginning, my senior year was even better than I'd hoped it would be, and the foundation of it all was the stable, warm, fun, but no-nonsense home Hugh and Mom Kat provided for me. I'd always wanted to have siblings, and living with two brothers helped me make the most of that time as a kid on the cusp of stepping into adulthood.

Sleeping on the couch one day, I was awakened when Tommy jumped in the air, crashed down on me, and kneed me in the gut. I rolled off the couch and pinned the kid to the floor. I shoved a dirty sock in his face and made him cry for mercy.

That kind of scene happens in houses all over the world every single day. No one pays attention to them, except maybe for the parents who come in and yell at the boys to take it outside or warn them that they'd better not break that lamp on the end table. But for me, it was one of the ways I knew I had become a part of the family. No one came in and said, "Ben, cut it out or you'll have to leave." I wasn't treated as a guest or a charity case. I was just family.

That acceptance even extended to the family dog, Bailey, a friendly Labrador retriever. Maybe it was because he was the family's dog and I knew there was no chance he would be taken away, but for the first time since Lady, I let myself get attached to a dog again. I'd come home in the evenings and play fetch with Bailey in the yard. My life was even better than the "Cosby Show" life I'd dreamed of having. Cliff and Clair were too good to be true, but they never let their kids have a dog.

Everything was great at home, but I still had a promise to keep to my aunt and to myself to make the most of my last year of high school, personally and academically. I took my work seriously and still made time for fun. I had been a popular kid throughout high school, and in September, my class voted me homecoming king. It was a nice way to be recognized, and I let myself enjoy the attention, but the year was flying by, and before I knew it, the holiday season was approaching. It would be one of the best I'd had in a long time.

That Christmas, when the Hugheses sent out their family Christmas card, they included me in the photo. It meant more to me than almost any gift I'd ever found under the tree. This was the card that went out to all of their family and friends. It didn't have a little asterisk next to my name to read "Ben *foster son." There was no explanation about who this brown child was who had suddenly appeared next to the sons everyone knew. I was just there as a part of the family.

While Mom Kat made me feel like one of her own children, she was always conscious of where my mother fit in that equation. She presented herself to my mother as the second mom, so that my mother had no reason to feel threatened, and Mom Kat wasn't being disingenuous in that. She cared about my mother's well-being, and she showed it by helping my mother get to my games and by being available to listen to my mother when she needed to talk.

––––––––

The White House was a big family house that was often filled with people, food, talk, and laughter. Mom Kat's brother, Craig, who had some special needs, often came by, and he and I quickly formed a bond. I was always happy to see him, and it was nice to have one more family member who was happy to see Ben the kid, not just Ben the basketball player.

And then there was Grandpa Neal. He wasn't Mom Kat or Hugh's father. He had married into the family, but he was definitely a consistent grandfather figure. An older guy, he was a gardener, and he did sit-ups and push-ups every day and stayed very active. He was also one of the kindest people I'd ever met.

When I had an important science project to do, Grandpa Neal volunteered to help. I needed to pull together a bug collection, and he was already a collector, so he was glad to show me the process, which started with finding, catching, and killing the bugs. Of course, I couldn't kill the bugs the way you do when you just want to get rid of a little pest. The body had to be preserved for display, and he showed me how to do that.

Grandpa Neal walked me through all the steps to create an impressive insect collection and earn a great grade on my assignment. It had been a long time since I'd had a grandfatherly presence like him to spend time with, and my relationship with my own grandfather had centered much more on sports. I appreciated Grandpa Neal's putting forth the effort to help me make something much better than I could have done on my own, but even more, I appreciated the time we had together.

One of the biggest stresses for high school seniors is the college application process. Most kids spend the year pulling their hair out, hoping they'll get in somewhere and then figuring out how to pay for it. Luckily for me, the process was easier because of my success in basketball. My financial circumstances dictated that I wasn't going anywhere that didn't offer me a full scholarship. I needed tuition, room, and board covered because there was no college fund growing in a bank account somewhere and waiting for me to tap into it. University of Minnesota-Duluth came through with exactly what I needed, and I accepted their offer. The pressure was off.

Our basketball team had a great year, and so did I. Our community supported us, and that year, more than twenty-five news articles were written about our team, many of which featured my exploits. After a game in which I scored forty points, one January headline read, "Raymond Shocks Ghosts." I still loved winning, and I enjoyed getting those kinds of public accolades. It was a great way to close out my career as a high school athlete.

Our community rallied around sports, and one of my classmates, Matt Hathaway, was a huge sports fan. He had some special needs, but he always had a smile on his face so that I couldn't help but smile back whenever I saw him. Matt lived in the neighborhood my mother and I had lived in when I was in eighth grade, and I remembered seeing him around when I went to that side of the neighborhood to play basketball. Some people picked on him, but the more I saw Matt around school the more I liked him. I'd pass him in the hallway, give him a high-five, and tease him about his favorite team. "Brewers suck, Matt!"

Matt would get mad, but it became a running joke between the two of us, and the guy with special needs and the homecoming king developed a friendship most people wouldn't have expected. I had become popular because of sports, but I still understood what it felt like to be an outsider, and when time for prom rolled around, I wanted to make sure Matt felt like he was on the inside with the rest of us.

That year, a group of eight of us seniors planned to go to the prom together. I talked to everyone and told them I wanted to add a ninth member to our party. Everyone was on board, and we invited Matt to go to the prom with us. We spent the night showering him with attention and making him feel like he was our own prom king. The girls danced with him, and the guys joked around with him. No one treated him like the token extra. We all treated him as a friend. Prom was a good time, of course, but seeing the joy on Matt's face made it a thousand times better.

Just like prom night was over before I knew it, my senior year in high school raced by in a blur of schoolwork, basketball games, dates, and hanging out with my friends. At the end of it all, I was proud of myself. I had kept my commitment to be a focused student, a committed athlete, and the best person I could be as I wrapped up high school.

My mother and her family attended my graduation, but they didn't attend the graduation party Hugh and Mom Kat threw for me at their house. Aunt Bonnie had stopped dealing with Mom Kat after the incident with the promise ring. I took it personally that she would disrespect the family that had taken me in, on a day that was really important to me and to them, and it damaged our relationship as aunt and nephew. I began to see her as someone who had to have her way and would hold grudges if you didn't go along with her. And I didn't like it.

The party went on without them, and as much as it was a celebration of my accomplishments it was also a celebration of everyone who had helped me along the way. We invited Matt to attend my graduation party, and he seemed to have a great time hanging out with me and my friends once again. At the end of the night, his parents expressed their gratitude to me for reaching out to make their son feel like a part of our class. "You didn't have to do that," they said. What they didn't understand was that it meant as much to me as it did to him. The Hughes family had given me a much-needed sense of belonging at one of my lowest points. If I could pay that forward even a little bit to my friend Matt, then I was the lucky one.

CHAPTER TEN

When you fully commit, you've already won.

High school was behind me, but I still had the whole summer stretched out in front of me before I'd start my freshman year at University of Minnesota. I was looking forward to some time to chill out and hang with my friends before we all went off in different directions. Chad was still my closest friend, and he and I were spending a lot of time together. We stayed up until two or three in the morning, playing video games and talking trash. Frankly, that was all I wanted to do for the summer, but there was a really simple rule at the Hughes family home. As Hugh said, "You have to have a job if you're going to live here."

That meant I was going to work, like it or not, but Hugh made it easy for me. He already had a job lined up for me with friends of his who owned a company that manufactured and applied industrial paints, sealants, and coatings. The job was even less exciting than it sounds. It was dirty, smelly factory work. Every day, I put on my overalls, boots, and mask and went in to work the second shift, and every day I came home filthy. Bailey, the Hughes family's dog, would lick the top layer of dirt off me when I got home, and a long, hot shower took care of the rest.

Most of the guys on the job were there for life, and some of them were annoyed at the temp workers like me who were just passing through. One of the factory workers, a man with a huge belly that swayed in front of him when he walked, voiced his distaste for us every single day. "You little college boys come into town, think you got it all figured out, don't you? Well, you ain't got shit figured out!"

Since I knew I wouldn't be there for long, I could ignore those comments, but I still hated that job. I was standing over five-hundred-gallon mixers, doing manual labor all day, and I was not into it.

One day, I pulled up for my shift to find the parking lot filled with fire trucks and ambulances. Red and blue lights strobed over the property, making it look like a crime scene. I got out of my car and asked one of the men what had happened.

"Guy got burned up," he said.

It turned out there'd been an explosion. A man working the same platform I usually worked on had been burned over most of his body. I never found out the exact cause of the explosion, but I was done. I liked the people who owned the company, but I wasn't working there anymore.

Because the owners were friends of Hugh, my supervisors let me work in another area for a while, but it didn't take me long to find another job. I wasn't willing to risk my life for any job, but the bottom line was manual labor wasn't for me. It was a perfect lesson for me to learn before I went off to pursue my degree. If I wanted to work with my mind rather than my hands, I needed to perform in the classroom as much as I did on the basketball court.

———

When fall came around and the new school term started, Mom Kat, Hugh, and Tommy dropped me off at the university to start my freshman year. Rather than live in a dorm with all the athletes, I chose a room in one of the newer buildings with girls on even floors and guys on odd floors. I figured I'd see more girls that way, and I was right. My roommate was six-six just like me, and we had to squeeze our athletes' bodies into extra-long twin bunk beds like everybody else. Together we did what we could to decorate our small space and make it our own.

Having a family to move me into my dorm was a big deal for me. I'm sure many college students take it for granted and can't wait for their parents and kid brothers and sisters to clear out of there, but for a long time, I'd thought it was an experience I'd never get to have, and I appreciated every moment of it.

After I'd put away my clothes and shoes, books and notebooks, and pencils and pens, I sat down on the edge of my bed and opened a card Mom Kat had left for me. Inside, she had written about how grateful she was to have me in her life, and as I read the list of things she appreciated about our time together, I knew she meant every single word. She had already shown me how much she loved me with her actions, but it was still great to read the words. One line on the card got right to the heart of our relationship, and I would never forget it. "Once single threads," Mom Kat had written, "we are now woven into a cable so strong that nothing can break or tear its beauty . . . We are family!"

In the weeks before coming to college, the voices of my doubters had occasionally crept into my head. I'd always been the kind of student who could earn a B without much effort, and some of my relatives thought I needed more academic discipline before I went to college. I had buckled down and put in a lot more effort during my senior year, but that hadn't stopped the warnings that I wasn't ready to handle college material. Every once in a while, for just a fleeting moment, I'd wonder if they were right about me. The future looked both promising and scary. I was excited for this new phase of my life, but I also had moments of worry, and Mom Kat's card helped me put all of that aside. She not only believed in me and knew I could make something of my life, but she would also be there for me if I ever need a place to fall.

I liked to think Mom Kat knew how much she and the rest of the Hughes family meant to me, but she couldn't have imagined how deeply those words would affect me. In their home, I had found what I'd spent years trying to find or create. It would have been easy to wish I'd moved in with them years earlier, but I'd arrived at the White House in God's perfect timing. I had been so angry and defensive for much of my adolescence that I'd closed myself off to some of the people who'd tried the best ways they knew how to reach me. By the time I arrived on Mom Kat's doorstep, I was a broken kid, but I was open to healing, and Mom Kat knew exactly what I needed to put the pieces back together.

Sitting there alone, holding that card in my hands, I looked back on the last decade of fighting to keep my life on track, struggling to force my mother to recognize when she needed help and actually go and get it, trying to protect her from herself and the company she kept, watching her go in and out of the hospital and wondering how long her recovery would last each time, searching for a home where I would feel safe and loved—all while my resentment for my absentee father grew.

I saw myself living with the Schade family, and the Nesbitt family, and the Hughes family, staying with my grandparents whenever my mother couldn't take care of me, and living with the Millers, who wanted to adopt me as a toddler. I'd bounced from home to home, and even though I finally found something really special with Mom Kat and the Hughes, it had come at the cost of separating from my mother, who I could never save from her depression, paranoia, mania, and drug addiction, no matter how hard I tried.

As I felt the weight of those years slip from my shoulders, I broke down. My body shook with tears that flowed not out of sadness but out of a sense of relief and freedom. I had struggled against my family history for so long and fought for the opportunity to create my own destiny, and for the first time in my life, I was truly the captain of my own ship. I was in control of my life. All of the drama was behind me. Every decision, from that point forward, would be my own to make. I was free. For almost an hour, I let myself cry, releasing all the pain and sadness that had been pent up inside of me for so long, celebrating the end of one long journey and the beginning of another.

———

I had watched plenty of college basketball on television, and I'd been around the university players in Oshkosh since I was a little kid, so I walked into my first practice as a collegiate athlete fully aware that there would be plenty of strong players. I wasn't expecting walk in and dominate from day one, but taking the court with a bunch of seniors who'd been hitting the weight room for four years made it very clear, very quickly, that this was a grown man's game. I wasn't playing with high school boys anymore. Luckily, I liked a challenge, and years of being the first to get to practice and last to leave had taught me that if I worked hard enough, I could keep up with almost anybody.

As far as academics went, Grace Lutheran had laid a strong foundation for me even before I got to high school. If I was ever tempted to slack off, I would hear the voices of people like Mr. Koepke who insisted I value my brain as much as my brawn. I would think about the workers back in the paint factory. Basketball had gotten me to college, but it would be up to me to make that mean something. I chose a double major in business management and marketing. Balancing my course load with practices and games was almost easy for me since I'd been playing year-round sports and managing my schoolwork since middle school. I knew how to manage my time.

And then there was the college social life. Early in my freshman year, I jumped into the party scene on campus. After watching the way drugs affected my mother and her boyfriends over the years, I had no desire to smoke, snort, shoot, or pop anything. I couldn't stand the idea of throwing my life away like that. It looked stupid to me. But I did want to have fun, and beer was the big drink at college parties. The only problem was that I didn't actually like the taste of it. Brown liquor made me act like an ass, so that was out too. For the most part, I filled my red plastic cup with wine coolers and fruity cocktails. It wasn't what you'd expect a big athlete to drink, but I liked drinks that tasted good. In between basketball and class, I found plenty of time to party.

Young people are often told to enjoy their college years because they'll be the best years of your life. I didn't plan for that to be true—I still had a lot I wanted to experience and enjoy in life after college—but I definitely enjoyed my college years. It was almost impossible not to have fun when I was living in the dorms. There was always something to get into. When we couldn't find anything else to do, a bunch of us played Tecmo Bowl, a football video game, on Nintendo game systems, and I was happy to take money from whoever thought they could beat me. I competed in those games like I was back on the field. It was a great way to pay for pizza.

Dorm life also came with a lot of pranks. Usually, it was simple, harmless stuff, like putting pennies in a door to lock someone in their room. However, on one occasion, the prank we pulled on one of the R.A.s, which seemed harmless to us, could have gotten us put out of school.

Most of the resident assistants were pretty cool. Unless we really crossed the line, they didn't hassle us, and we returned the favor by giving them respect when they did have to address an issue. However, there was one R.A. in the dorm who seemed to think it was her personal duty to make sure nobody had any fun. She was always looking for something to call us out on. She was a miserable person who wanted company in her misery, and nobody liked her.

One day, a few of us were sitting around talking about something she'd done, and I suggested we should prank her while she was out. "You know what we should do?" I said. "We should fill her room with crickets."

Everybody was on board, but I let a couple of other guys handle the dirty work. I was happy to come up with the idea, but I wasn't trying to get caught in the act.

Needless to say, the R.A. came home to an unpleasant surprise, and she immediately suspected we'd done it. There were so many crickets in her room that she had to be moved to another dorm until maintenance could de-cricket her room. I like to think it was a win-win. She was probably as happy to get away from us as we were to see her to go.

————

When Mom Kat claimed me as family, she meant it, and when holidays and summer breaks rolled around and it was time to go home, I went home to the White House. Going home that first summer, I knew for sure that I needed to find a job, but I also got to experience my first real family vacation.

That summer, the Hughes family, which now included me, went on a vacation to Colorado. It was a long drive in the family's Explorer from Wisconsin to Beaver Creek, outside of Vail. I was going nuts being trapped in the car for more than a thousand miles, and as we got closer to Colorado, Tommy was freaking out as we drove along winding roads with what looked to us like sheer drops off the mountain side. It was a typical "Are we there yet?" ride with kids getting grumpy and sick of each other, and as much as I complained, I loved every minute of it.

We went mountain biking, flying down steep hills, and hiked the trails. To me, it was the kind of vacation television families went on. That same year, I traveled to Disney World and Universal Studios, in Orlando, Florida, for a basketball tournament. That was exciting, but I'd been traveling for sports since I was in fourth grade. A family vacation had been one of my boyhood dreams, and Hugh and Mom Kat had made it come true.

Back at home after our Colorado trip, I went to work, but I also went in to party mode. I took advantage of every opportunity to hang out with old friends. It had only been a year since we all graduated high school, and old attachments were easily picked back up when we all came home for the summer. On the Fourth of July, Evan and I went to a barbecue. Even though I knew I wasn't a beer drinker, I got caught up in the festivities and had more than my fair share of beer and food. On the way home, all of it mixed and churned in my stomach until I knew what was going to happen. Everything I had consumed was coming back up, and I wasn't going to make it to a bathroom.

I found a place in the backyard, a spot where no one would ever go and no one would ever see me, and I threw up there. Then I stumbled into bed and passed out.

Just a few hours later, I hear Hugh yelling at Evan. "What the hell? Have you been drinking?"

Evan sprung up with a fast "No!" even though he had definitely been drinking just like I was. The difference was he hadn't left any evidence behind.

The next thing I knew, Hugh was standing over my bed. "Ben, have you been drinking? Did you throw up in the yard?"

I had only been asleep a few hours, and I still could have blown the meter off a breathalyzer. "Yeah," I said.

"Get outside and clean that mess up right now!" Hugh shouted at me. "The dog's been in it!"

Bailey was a great dog, but he'd gotten me busted.

———

I still loved playing basketball, and I learned a lot of valuable lessons from my college coach about how to build an organization and foster teamwork. If somebody on the team had been skipping class, he put him to the side and let him stand there and watch the rest of us run until we were ready to drop. After that, we'd still have to do a full practice, and we'd all be ready to kill the guy who screwed up in the first place. Needless to say, there weren't a lot of repeat offenders.

My college basketball career started off well, but by the end of my sophomore year, I was getting frustrated. I had gotten a lot of playing time during my freshman year, but in my sophomore year, I saw teammates I was dominating getting more time than the coach gave me. I couldn't understand it. I wasn't giving any less than I'd given as a freshman. It felt completely unfair, and by the end of the season, I was ready to quit.

But I had never quit anything like that, and it would've been a stupid move. I was getting a free education out of this deal. At the end of the year, I pulled my coach aside for an honest conversation.

"I don't like the way things are going," I said. "What do I have to do to play more? I want to know exactly what you need from me so I can take over the position."

He listed off specific things he wanted to see from me.

I told him, "If I execute all of those things, then I want to know you'll give me fair shake, because if you do, I know I'll win that position."

The coach agreed. He was a man of his word, and so was I. I came back and not only started in every game from that point on, I was also captain of the team for my junior and senior years.

I didn't like the way my coach did a lot of things, but in the end, it turned out to be a test of what I was made of and how bad I wanted to be out there playing. I could have sat back and said, "Oh, well, I guess I don't have what he's looking for." I could have quit. I could have developed a bad attitude or challenged his authority. In hindsight, I'm glad I took the right path and finished my time as a collegiate athlete with integrity.

As much as I loved my time on the court, I was realistic about the fact that I didn't have a future as a pro basketball player. Only about one percent of male college basketball players go on to play in the NBA. I had already beaten the odds by going as far as I had. Only three percent of high school basketball players who play in their senior year end up playing college ball, and only two percent of high school athletes are awarded any amount athletic scholarships to help cover the cost of their college education.

Everyone has to find what they're good at, the thing that sets them apart and can open doors for them in life. For some, it might be math or writing, artistic ability, music, acting, or something completely out of the box. For me, that door-opener had been basketball, and it had served me well. I had no regrets about my years in sports or how much of my time and energy I'd committed to making the most of my athletic potential. Yes, like so many young athletes, I'd once harbored dreams of playing in the pros, but I recognized that basketball had already given me so much in return for what I'd put into it, and I was grateful.

———

Even though she'd been an honor student in high school, my mother's mental illness had made it impossible for her to complete her bachelor's degree. Her father, my grandfather, had dropped out of high school to go to work. I didn't know my father, but I knew he hadn't gotten a degree either. I hadn't grown up in a home where a college education was a given. In fact, all along the way, people had doubted my ability to go to college and graduate with a degree. I was the child of a single mother who struggled with mental illness and drug addiction and a man who'd been in and out of jail and also battled addiction. I had lived in a home where my mother had been a victim of domestic violence, and when it became too much, I'd relied on other families to

take me in and bounced from one house to another and back again.
I wasn't supposed to make it.

Graduating with a dual degree in business management and marketing made me feel like anything was possible for me. I had defied
the naysayers time and again, and I would keep doing it for the rest
of my life. When graduation day rolled around, I was on top of the
world. My mom and Derrel, the Hugheses and Chad, Aunt Bonnie,
Uncle Jack, and my cousin Stephanie all sat in the stands as my name
was called and I crossed the stage to receive my the piece of paper that
certified me as a college graduate. For years, people had cheered for
my feats on the basketball court, and I'd loved every minute of it. But
hearing them applaud my academic achievement meant even more.

As my family and friends hugged me and congratulated me, I
tried to take it all in, but I also wondered what the moment would be
like if my father were there too. He'd missed all of the most important
moments in my life—from championship games to high school graduation and now this—and I couldn't help wondering if my journey
might have been easier if he'd been there to guide me. Would I have
accomplished more, faster? Would I have been able to turn to him
for advice when I was thinking of quitting basketball or as I went out
into the world to find a job that let me put my degree to good use?
For a long time, I had pushed away my curiosity about my father,
but on that day, a day I'd worked for years to get to, I couldn't help
imagining what it would have been like to have him there.

PHOTOGRAPHS

My wife, Karli, our son, BJ, and me. New Year's Eve 2016

My mother, Nancy Raymond. Senior portrait. Beaver Dam High School

My mother and me on the day of my baptism

My mother and me at my college graduation

My mother and me at my wedding

My toddler years

My first Christmas portrait

Fox Valley Wildcats, age 11

Camera Casino soccer, after three goals

Quarterback for the
North Eagles, 7th grade

My senior portrait with my
trophies and awards

Left:

My first Hughes family Christmas

Below:

Mom Kat and me on a "Mother's Day - Thank You" episode of the Steve Harvey daytime talk show

The Hughes family at my college graduation: Tom, Evan, me, Mom Kat, Hugh

My father, Slim, and me at a Dallas
Cowboys game. December 2012

Out to dinner with my father

My sister, Davida, and me.
September 2016

My niece, Aniah, me, and Davida.
Disney Dreamers. March 2017

My beautiful wife, Karli, and me. Engagement photos.

Our wedding day. September 26, 2015

My stepdad Derrel, my mother Nancy, Karli, and me.

Karli and me, Capetown, South Africa. March 2016

Karli and me. London, England.
March 2016

BJs first Christmas

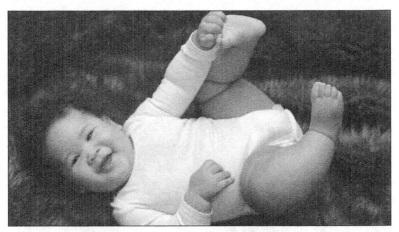

Benjamin Troy Raymond II. Age: 6 months.

BJ, at 2 months old,
with his proud father

BJ, in Anguilla for Pawpaw's
60th birthday

BJ at NBC Studios Chicago.
May 2017

60th birthday episode
for my father-in-law

Close friends and business associates join me on my wedding day

My groomsmen and me: Terry Moore, Tareq Humphrey, Elmer Barnes IV, Damione Liddell, Broderick Harvey (Karli's younger brother)

My friend and mentor, Al Sicard, and me. September 2016

Sharing my story with the kids

"You Can Be Me" Mentoring Panel. February 2017

CHAPTER ELEVEN

You don't get what you wish for;
you get what you work for.

I stared into my empty refrigerator—nothing but sports drinks and leftover Chinese food on the shelves—while I pressed the phone to my ear. "I'm not going to make it home for a while," I told Mom Kat. "You know I've been fighting this flu."

The small stack of bills on the kitchen counter caught my eye and distracted me from what she was saying. I faked a cough and wrapped up our conversation.

I was running out of excuses to put off Mom Kat, my mom, and anyone else who asked when I was coming home to visit. This time, I told everyone I couldn't make it because I'd been sick, but I was lying to protect my pride. In truth, I didn't have enough money to put gas in my luxury SUV to make the four-and-a-half hour drive.

The scholarship that had carried me through college ended when I graduated weeks earlier. I still had to pay my rent and utilities and buy food. Like so many college students, I had fallen deep into the trap of credit card debt. To top it all off, and I had to make the payments on the Land Rover Discovery I'd bought myself as a graduation present, back when I was sure I'd finish college with multiple job offers laid out for me. Ready or not, I had stepped fully into the world of adult responsibilities. All of that would've been manageable except I still didn't have a job to match those financial commitments.

I grabbed the bills and took them with me to the living room, where I dropped onto the sofa and clicked on the television to try to find something to take my mind off of my finances. I flipped from channel to channel, but watching TV just reminded me of the cable bill, which was already overdue.

While some of my peers went off to start their corporate careers, I was still slinging electronics at Best Buy. I could sell any product on the floor, from TVs and DVD players to laptops and game systems. I enjoyed talking to customers and matching the right product with the right person. I read up on new merchandise so I could answer any questions or objections a customer had. I was a top sales associate, but the job was a dead end for me.

The recession was hurting job prospects for a lot of graduates, and increasingly, young people who couldn't find employment were moving back home to live with their parents until they could figure out their next move. That was never going to work for me. I was never going to live under my mother's roof again, especially not a roof that belonged to her and Derrel. I had worked too hard to escape a lifestyle that included their on-again, off-again drug use, Derrel going in and out of jail, and whatever schemes they had going on. There was no going back to that instability and drama.

I could have moved home with the Hughes family, but that wouldn't solve my problem. I'd still have to find a job. Sure, it might have been easier for me to get work back in Oshkosh. I knew plenty of people there, and Hugh had friends who owned businesses and would give me a shot as a favor to him. My high school glory days on the basketball court had left me well connected and well liked in the community too. Someone would hire me.

Landing a job in Oshkosh wouldn't be a problem, but it also wouldn't put me on a professional career track. I was ready to earn some real money and stop living like a broke-ass college student. I was ready for a job with plenty of earning potential and opportunities to grow. Besides, there was nothing I wanted to return to in my home town. There were too many bad memories of dark days in Oshkosh, and I'd never felt like I fit in there. Ultimately, I was ready to stand on my own two feet and build a life of my own.

There was no escaping the reality of my nearly empty checking account or the debt I was accumulating. I opened the small white envelope that rested on top of the others, a credit card bill. Forget about the outstanding balance. Looking at the numbers, I realized that by the time I made the minimum payment and paid my rent, I'd barely have enough cash left over to stock my cabinet with three-for-a-dollar ramen and hit the McDonald's drive-thru for breakfast on the way to work. It was the final straw. I was tired of scrambling for money. I'd studied hard for four years, pushed myself to graduate with not one but two degrees, played basketball every year, and worked a full-time job every summer. I wanted the reward I'd envisioned for myself at the end of all that hard work and sacrifice.

But I needed help to get there.

Asking for money was the last thing I wanted to do. I had a huge chip on my shoulder because so many people who I'd thought were in my corner had started to doubt me, but I was going to have to get over it. The one person in a position to lend me the kind of money I needed was my aunt. I'd grown up spending holidays with Aunt Bonnie and her family at my grandparents' house, every year, when my mother would inevitably go back into treatment. After my grandfather died, my aunt had often stepped in to fill the gap my grandfather had once filled for my mother and me when money ran short. I'd always felt like my aunt was in my corner.

However, in recent months, Aunt Bonnie had questioned why in the world I was still working at Best Buy instead of finding a "real job." More than once, she implied that I was wasting my education, and she even had my mother doubting if I'd ever get my life together. Aunt Bonnie knew as well as anyone how impressionable my mother was. It didn't take much to influence her, and Aunt Bonnie's comments about how I needed to stop fooling around were more than sufficient to push my mother into worry, fear, and nonstop questions about my plans for survival.

I slid the credit card bill back into the envelope, picked up my laptop, and opened my email. I would have loved to prove to Aunt Bonnie and everyone else putting me down that I could figure things out and get my career moving on my own, but the fact was that I was in a hole, and I was tired of trying to claw my way out only to find myself sliding back down again.

My trouble with Aunt Bonnie hadn't just started with my failure to launch from graduation right into a professional position. The two of us had fallen out after I took over management of my mother's trust during my senior year of college. While she managed the trust, my aunt had struggled to deal with my mother's day-to-day ups and downs. Nobody could blame her. If my mother didn't take her medication regularly or if she happened to be using again, you could never tell which Nancy you would get. She might be depressed and withdrawn and thinking the world was out to get her, or she might be so manic that she'd call you twenty times a day, talking excitedly about something that made absolutely no sense to anyone but her.

Because my mother loved me deeply and wanted to make me happy, it was easier for me to convince her to make better decisions than she might otherwise make. I could rattle some sense into my mom even when nobody else could, but I didn't manage things the way Aunt Bonnie had. If I was going to take on the responsibility of the trust, then I meant to do it my way, and I did. My decisions had caused a lot of friction between my aunt and me, but whatever our differences were, I hoped she could see past them. There was only one way to find out.

I started typing. "Aunt Bonnie, I hope you still believe in me and you're not losing confidence in me like so many other people are," I wrote. I explained that I was still making an aggressive job search, but I was running short on cash.

"I want to get two new interview suits and a cover a few other expenses," I wrote. "If you can loan me seven hundred dollars, I promise you I'll pay you back as soon as I land the right position."

I understood how important image was, especially in a highly competitive job market. I needed to dress not like a recent graduate looking for his first job but like a successful man who already had the job I wanted. I needed the money to make that investment in myself, and if that meant paying my aunt back with interest, I would. "I'll pay you back double if that's what you want," I wrote.

It took everything I had to nudge that chip off my shoulder long enough to push send on the email, but I did it. And Aunt Bonnie came through for me again. Underneath her doubts, she must have still had enough faith to take a chance on me. She loaned me the money, and it was game on.

———

With my new infusion of cash, I went out and bought two of the sharpest suits I could afford. They were just what I needed to give me the look I wanted for my interviews, the kinds of suits I could feel good wearing when I walked into a human resources office or when I sat across the desk from company vice presidents who asked what I thought I could contribute to their bottom line, how I would handle a potential buyer's objections, or whether or not I was a Packers fan living in Vikings country.

I was going after sales positions because I already knew I was good at getting the yes. Not only did I shine in my retail job, but one of my marketing professors had pointed out that I was tailor-made for sales. After I'd given a product line presentation in his class, he'd pulled me aside and told me I had a gift. "You have a presence," he told me. "You command the room without even trying. Don't take that for granted. You could do incredibly well in sales." I didn't exactly know how to follow his advice at the time, but I never forgot his words of encouragement.

During college, I'd also done an internship with Lamar Advertising, the company responsible for more than 300,000 of the billboards that sprung up out of the landscapes of cities and towns across North America. In my short tenure with the century-old company, I was exposed to different facets of a large, publicly traded corporation, and I saw firsthand how crucial the sales force was to the bottom line. The idea of earning commissions on top of my base salary excited me. I knew I could max it out because I was more than willing to do the hard work it took to be a top performer.

So many people were intimidated by the idea of selling, but the challenge appealed to me. I liked the clear-cut nature of sales numbers. In basketball you either scored or you didn't. You won or you lost; there was no gray area. In sales, you either met or exceeded your goals, meaning you won, or you didn't, and you lost. There was no question about whether you were performing or not. Anyone could look at the stats and see who was doing what.

I signed on with a recruiting firm that specialized in placing college athletes with top companies around the country. These corporations had caught on to the fact that the same skills that helped us succeed in athletics could make us superstars on their teams. Within a few weeks, I'd landed a position that would make the haters sit down and shut up for once and for all.

———

In fall of 2002, I went to work for Cintas Corporation, in Minneapolis. The company sold and serviced uniforms, floor mats, safety products, and much of the supplies a business with a public face needs to run but which few customers ever think about. Most importantly, Cintas was a Fortune 500 company with an excellent commission structure.

One of the most important lessons I'd learned in sports and from living with the Hughes family was that to be on time was to be late, and I took that principle with me to the workplace. On my first day at Cintas, I got up early, put on a suit that made me look like a winner, and hopped in my car with plenty of time to walk through the office doors well before I was due to start work.

As I was backing out of the alley behind my house, I felt my car's rear-end smack into something solid, and I slammed on the brakes. I'd run right into another vehicle.

I quickly exchanged insurance information with the driver, but I was at a loss as to what to do next. Hugh was the one person I knew who had succeeded in the business world, and since he also worked in insurance, I knew he'd give me the best advice on what to do about the accident and about my first day at work. I called him and explained what had happened.

"You let her leave?" he asked. "You idiot! You don't have any witnesses. Now, it's your word against hers. She could run into a light pole on the way to work and sue you for the damages!"

I shook my head. I hadn't even thought of that. "So what am I supposed to do now?"

"You get your ass to work!" Hugh shouted through the phone. "And you get there on time!"

I did get there on time, and even though the morning hadn't started the way I wanted it to, the rest of the day went well. It seems like such a small thing now, but getting my first business cards with my name embossed on them made me feel like a legitimate professional. It was a proud moment for me. It was three-and-a-half-by-two-inch representation of my success.

Now that I had the job and I had managed to get to work, I was ready to hit the ground running. I was hungry to start selling and earning commissions. I wanted to show everyone what I could do, but my manager put the brakes on my excitement. Before I could go on sales calls, I had to rotate through the other parts of the business, including riding with the delivery truck drivers and working in the plant.

They started me off working with a guy who made eight dollars an hour rolling mats. I jumped in next to him with enthusiasm, but inside, I was grumbling. I hadn't fought my way to this job so I could end up doing manual labor. I respected that someone had to do it, but I didn't want that someone to be me.

I asked the man I was working with, an immigrant from an African country, "So you do this same thing for seven hours every day?"

"Yeah," he said, "and then I go home and change clothes, have a quick dinner, and go to my other job."

"You have two jobs?" I asked.

"I work at the yogurt factory too, a full-time shift. I'm saving money to bring my wife here from Africa." He kept working as we talked.

As I listened to his story of immigrating to America in search of opportunity for his family and himself, I felt like the most ungrateful person in the world. This man was working sixteen-hour days, on his feet all day, in two jobs with very little potential for him to grow into something less taxing. And I dared to complain, even to myself, about spending a few hours working in the plant? I was proud of my own drive and dedication, but his could stand next to mine on any day.

This was a man who understood the power of short-term sacrifice for long-term gain. I lived by the principle that you don't get what you wish for; you get what you work for. This was a man who lived by that same principle in a very real way, and he earned my admiration on that day. In the months that followed, we became friends. There was no one in that company I thought more highly of or respected more. Even though I lost touch with him after I left Cintas, I'm sure he went on to do well for himself. I'm not a gambler, but I'd be willing to bet that he accomplished his goal and brought his wife to live with him in the United States. Failure wasn't an option for him. He was a man of focus and determination, and what he put his mind to he would achieve.

———

It was my first full-time, corporate job, and I took it on the way I took on every other challenge in my life. Once I finished my orientation and training, I came out of the gate fast. Within my first quarter at Cintas, I was breaking records. I sold a thirty-location contract to a chain of oil-change specialty shops. I sold an account to the Minnesota Wild, a National Hockey League team. I was "Rookie of the Quarter" for the Midwest and among the top five in the country, and my confidence went through the roof. I'd gone from counting my pennies to finally having some disposable income.

As my career took off, so did my social life. Outside of work, I was hitting the clubs, meeting lots of women, and just having a good time living the life of a bachelor with some money in his wallet. The financial pressure I'd felt for years was finally gone, and I enjoyed that freedom. I also stuck to my word and repaid Aunt Bonnie's loan with my first check. The satisfaction I got from proving myself to anyone and everyone who had wondered if I was really going to make something of myself was priceless.

I was killing it in my job, so when my manager pulled me aside one day, I just knew there was nothing he could criticize in my performance.

"I wanted to talk to you about something real quick, Ben," he said as he shut his office door.

"Absolutely," I said. "What's going on?"

"Well, I understand that you have your own sense of style, but I just want to give you a heads-up that this is really a white shirt kind of company. You know what I mean?" His message was clear: don't think you're so good that you don't have to fit in like the rest of us.

I glanced down at my pink dress shirt. "Understood," I said.

"White shirt," he repeated, "and a dark suit, and you'll be fine."

That was the end of our meeting on dress code, and even though I said I understood what he was saying, I thought it was ridiculous. Yes, I had my own sense of style, but fashion had always been my thing, and I knew how to stand out with a little flair and still be professional. I didn't quite grasp that at a large, conventional corporation, standing out isn't always a good thing. I told myself I'd just have to light up the sales scoreboard even more. Then they'd have to let me wear whatever I wanted.

I had a lot to learn about corporate culture, but I wasn't sure I wanted to learn it. While something as simple as what to wear to work might not be a big deal to most employees, it flipped a switch for me. It was the beginning of my realization that I wanted to be a business owner one day. I wasn't sure how or when yet, but it was an idea that would stick with me, and every new constraint on my freedom would intensify my desire to launch a business that let me make those decisions for myself.

But for the time being, I was a sales rep for Cintas, and I continued to keep my name in the top of the sales rankings. I got over the need to dress the way I wanted and got into an efficient routine that actually allowed me to hit my numbers and have time left over at the end of the day. I could have found something productive to do with the extra time, but frankly, I got a little lazy. The job wasn't challenging me. I could go into the field, make my sales, and go home and kick it for the rest of the day. Even when I slacked off, I was still a top performer, hitting over five times the quota the company had set for me.

I was signing six-figure deals and making a lot of money for the company, which was what I was hired to do, but I was putting up numbers that equaled what four or five guys together might put up in the same month. In my first year on the sales force, I was one of the top five sales people in the country, and all of that success only made me want more.

———

The same way I'd push myself to be the best in sports, I drove myself hard to max out my commission. I did incredibly well, but I hadn't really thought about the reality of what it would feel like to make more money than I'd ever earned before—more than my mother had ever made at one time. When my first commission check arrived, I was completely unprepared for it. What was I supposed to do with a check for almost ten thousand dollars?

I thought back to all the times when my mother and I shopped for clothes at Goodwill because that was the best she could afford to give me. I thought about the way she'd sacrificed and humbled herself to borrow money to make sure I could go on those trips with my travel teams. I thought about how, no matter how far into depression or mania her bipolar disorder dragged her or how far she slid into drug use, she always fought her way back to be there for me.

There's a reason why you see so many black athletes take their first big pay day and buy their mothers a new car or even a new house. Like I was, so many of them are raised by single mothers, these courageous women who do everything in their power to try to fill the roles of both mother and father for us. Our mothers delay their own dreams and pour everything they have into helping us secure ours. They give up the luxuries they'd love to have for themselves so we can get a new pair of sneakers, a summer at sports camp, or an address in the right school district.

With the money from my first commission check, I wanted to honor my mother too. Instead of buying her a gift, I planned a trip so we could spend time together. It was the kind of family vacation I'd always wanted to go on with her, and I felt tremendous pride in being able to do that for her. We traveled to Tampa, where we hung out at the beach, enjoying the Florida sun. I treated my mother to some time in a spa and nice meals in the best restaurants. Seeing her free from the stress of her daily life, even if just for a few days, was worth every moment of my fight to climb out of poverty.

I also took my mother to see the Green Bay Packers play the Tampa Bay Buccaneers on that trip. We were both Packers fans, and it was a special treat to take the woman who'd watched games with me on television, since I was very small boy, to see our favorite team play in person. After the game, I went down to holler at some of the players I knew. My mother decided to walk around for a bit, and she planned to meet me at a pirate ship display we'd noticed earlier when I was done. It was a ship in the middle of a stadium. Who could miss it?

When I reached the team's security, I jokingly said I was one of the players, and they let me through. I shrugged and laughed to myself and went over to where the Packers were loading up their bus to leave the stadium. After I'd spoken to a few friends, I decided it was time to go, and I called my mother.

"Where are you?" I asked her.

"I can't find the ship," she said.

What my mother hadn't realized was that, as soon as the game was over, the pirate ship display came down. Our planned meeting spot didn't even exist anymore.

"Stay where you are," I told her. "I'll come to you."

But of course, my mother didn't stay where she was. The next hour was like a scene from a sitcom. Wherever my mother was, by the time I got there, she had moved on, looking for me. The stadium was huge, and we must have missed each other at least a dozen times. I could not get that woman to stay still for anything, but eventually, we ended up in the same place, greeting each other with laughter at the ridiculousness of it al. We might have lost each other for a moment, but as always, we'd managed to find our way back to each other. It had been a great day and a great trip.

Traveling to Tampa had been my idea of a special gift for my mother, but it also turned out to be a gift to myself. It gave me a serious travel bug that would eventually change the way I saw the world and my own life. For the first time, I began to see travel as an opportunity to expand my mind and be exposed to different things. I decided that since I was going to work hard, I would also reward myself with a chance to see a new part of the world every chance I could.

In the coming years, I'd walk the streets, paths, dirt roads, and beaches of lands that the little boy waiting at home alone, staring out at the darkness and wishing his life was different, never imagined he'd see. Between my vacation travel, mission work, and the trips I'd earn as a reward for top sales performance, I would visit the Commonwealth of Puerto Rico, the Czech Republic, Germany, England, France, Austria, Bermuda, the Bahamas, South Africa, Malawi, Senegal, Tanzania, Bali, Canada, Spain, France, Thailand, and other countries. As much as I enjoyed the luxury resorts and fine restaurants, my life would be forever changed by serving some of the poorest people on earth, people whose daily lives would inspire a new appreciation in me for everything I had. It would help me realize that, in the grand scheme of things, I'd never really known what it means to be poor, or thirsty, or hungry at all.

The commissions I earned at Cintas allowed me to begin to live out my dreams of traveling the world and to raise my lifestyle to a new level. One of the most meaningful examples of that lifestyle change was the purchase of my own home. During my first year out of college, my first year working in corporate America, I bought a three-bedroom, two-bath house in a nice neighborhood. I'd spent the first eighteen years of my life bouncing from one place to another, and there had even been times when I didn't know where I'd spend the night. Buying my own house was a huge accomplishment for me. It was the fulfillment of my dream to always have a place to call home, and I took great pride in finally becoming that handy guy who knew how to grab a toolbox and fix a leak or replace a cracked tile.

Working at Cintas definitely had its advantages. But I was going on sales calls to places like post offices, fast food restaurants, gas stations, and hotel chains. They weren't exactly the most glamorous or exciting locations. The products I sold were essential to any business, but they were also pretty boring. I started to get the itch to move on to something more challenging, more prestigious, and more fun.

When I'd graduated college, the job market had been tight, but after working for Cintas for a year and a half, I had a phenomenal sales record. In my first year, I'd made $40,000 in sales commissions, more than one hundred percent of my $35,000 base salary. Just like I'd loved seeing myself in highlight reels and reading my name in headlines when I played basketball, I loved seeing my name on awards and recognitions for sales. I still loved winning, and I knew I could exploit that passion to land an even better job.

Looking at the numbers also stirred the entrepreneurial spirit in me. Even though I was doing well as far as commissions, I was earning chump change compared to what I was bringing in for the company. I imagined what it would be like to be an owner and control the cash flow coming in, rather than taking my tiny percentage as a reward. I thought about how much I could earn and the impact I could have if I had my own company. I wasn't ready to make that kind of leap just yet, but I could see it in my future.

For the time being, I would still need to sell for someone else—something I'd proven I was one of the best at doing. If I put a contract in front a prospect, I had complete confidence that I'd walk away with a signature on the dotted line, and most of the time, I did just that. The good thing about sales is that once you learn how to sell one thing, you can sell anything. After a year at Cintas, it was time for me to go after that dream job, the elite class of sales positions. It was time for me to become a drug pusher.

CHAPTER TWELVE

You only have two options:
give up or give everything you've got.

Some time during my senior year of high school, my mother and her brother and sister had noticed that my grandmother's behavior seemed odd and unlike the woman they'd known since their childhood. She became forgetful and was easily confused. When the house started to smell because she'd stored cartons of milk in the kitchen cabinets, her children had to admit something was wrong with their mother. Doctors diagnosed my grandmother with late-stage Alzheimer's disease.

She had played an important role in my life almost since my birth, and the news hit me hard. Without my grandmother's help, it would've been nearly impossible for my mother to regain custody of me after I was placed in foster care as an infant. Whenever my mother was hospitalized during my childhood, my grandmother did her best to make my stays at her home as happy and as normal as possible. Dolores Raymond, my maternal grandmother, had been one of the few constants in my chaotic youth.

Once she received her diagnosis, my grandmother's doctor enrolled her in one of the early drug trials for treatment of Alzheimer's, one of the least understood and most debilitating diseases of the time. Unfortunately, it was too late for her. She continued to decline, and as her suffering increased, so did the suffering of all of us who loved her.

Watching someone you love slowly lose touch with the world around her is a pain I wouldn't wish on anyone. The disease affects a sufferer's ability to remember people and events, but it also diminishes her ability to solve problems and follow simple directions, leaving her less and less capable of taking care of herself. Finally, it destroys the brain connections that allow the patient to do the most basic things, like walk around on their own and feed themselves. Many patients die of malnutrition, dehydration, or aspiration pneumonia because they've been robbed of the capability to swallow food and water properly.

By the time I went to work for Cintas, my grandmother had struggled with Alzheimer's for almost five years. Whenever I visited her or got an update on her health, I was reminded that, while I definitely wanted to earn a good living, I also wanted to do work that felt like it meant something. My job at Cintas paid well, but I wanted to provide the world with something more than floor mats and uniforms. Those things mattered, and my sales equaled jobs for the plant workers, delivery truck drivers, and office staff, but it didn't have much meaning for me personally.

All through college, I'd heard business students talk about going into pharmaceutical sales. It paid well and also had a certain glamour to it, with fat expense accounts for reps to wine and dine doctors. While "big pharma" also had a reputation in some circles as being nearly predatory in its pursuit of profit, I'd seen firsthand the positive impact the right medication could have.

That kind of help may have come too late for my grandmother, but for my mother, taking her prescription, in the right dosage and at the right times, had meant the difference between raising her own child and losing him to foster care. It meant the difference between holding down a decent job and falling into a depression that kept her trapped in the house, afraid of whatever waited outside her front door. It meant the difference between living a normal life and feeling like she was going crazy.

———

I hadn't been at Cintas very long before I started thinking about moving on, and pharmaceutical sales seemed like the way to go. In previous generations, the road to success was a straight line. You joined one company, put in the work for decades, and slowly, with one small promotion every year or two, you climbed up the corporate ladder. But by the early 2000s, many professionals had figured out that the fastest way to get a pay increase was often to jump to another company. Where a resume that showed shorter time periods at different jobs used to look flaky, it had become an indication of ambition and aggressiveness in your career. I was ambitious and aggressive, and I was ready for a change.

In the spring of 2003, after working at Cintas for a year, I landed a position with Eli Lily, a global pharmaceutical company with headquarters in Indianapolis, Indiana. Right off the bat, my base salary went up by $20,000 a year, a big increase for a young man still in his twenties. It also felt good to be a part of the health care field and know that my work would play a small part in making someone's life better.

Initially, the job had all of the flash and excitement I'd expected. I had grabbed the holy grail of sales. I was taking physicians out to the best restaurants, which meant I got to enjoy some of the finest meals too. One day, I saw a homeless man on the corner near the restaurant where I was meeting a prospect, and at the end of the meal, I decided to bring out extra food for him. His surprise and gratitude made my day even more than the sale I'd closed.

It was the start of a new habit for me. After every meal, I'd order something to give to one of the homeless men or women in the area. I hoped it made a small difference to them to enjoy a quality meal but also to know someone dining in that fancy restaurant was thinking about them.

At Eli Lily, I worked on a sales team for a product called Evista, formulated to treat and prevent osteoporosis in women. We launched the product to doctors and health care professionals throughout the region. Later, I was on the team getting the word out about Cialis, a drug used to treat erectile dysfunction. It was actually a fun drug to sell. It solved a real problem, but this was the stuff sitcom one-liners and late-night spoofs were made of. The conversation with doctors was lighter and often hilarious, and I enjoyed doing my part to help Cialis take thirty-five percent of the market share.

Some of the jokes on the job weren't so funny though. One fall morning, I walked into the office, and a white coworker looked at me and said, "Oh, I guess you're here to fill the quota." He laughed it off, but I'd have to be stupid not to see his real feelings behind that jab. It certainly wasn't my first encounter with racism disguised as humor, but that didn't mean I liked it. Even though I'd earned the job based on my record as a top salesperson at Cintas, and I was killing at Eli Lily, it still irritated me that anyone thought I needed to prove I was more than a token.

I'd been conditioned for most of my life to be a loyal team player, but I was finding that there were sometimes different rules for making the team in corporate America. Getting cut could have less to do with poor performance and more to do with personality conflicts. I ran into one situation where nothing I could do would win a particular boss's favor.

She was an older white woman with children, and she singled out for preferential treatment the people who were most like her. I was a black man, single and child-free, and there was no room for me in the inner circle that made up her favorite team. When she doled out opportunities, they went to her friends first, and everyone else, including me, got the leftovers.

I wanted to believe business was business and everyone would be judged based on performance, but friendship came first with her. No matter how much effort I put in, she overlooked me time and time again. I felt so disrespected by her that it actually made me dead-set against working with women bosses for a while.

Once I got over my anger and realized her behavior had nothing to do with her gender, my experience gave me a new compassion for women in the professional world who run into roadblocks with the "old boys club" and have to fight to get ahead even when they're top performers. Giving your all to help the company profit and prosper, only to be shut out, is more than a little frustrating.

Not only did I fail to fit in with the working moms, I also couldn't join the party crowd. A lot of my coworkers went out together after work, and their idea of a good time always included lots of cocktails, wine, and beer. Even though they invited me to join them, I knew they would judge me by a different standard. If I went out with them on a Friday night, drank as much as they did, and made a general fool of myself, they'd look at me a lot differently on Monday morning. They'd all still be friends, and I'd be the drunk black guy. I knew that kind of socializing could be a career-ender for me. I still kicked it and had a good time. I just made sure I only did it in the company of coworkers or friends I could trust.

While I faced some obstacles with office personalities and politics, selling still came easily, and success made it easier to create my place in the company. I definitely enjoyed many of the benefits I'd expected to come with my new job too. The only problem with my new "dream job" was that, when it came down to it, I actually earned less than I'd made at Cintas. I was a top performer, but the commission checks were less than I'd made selling floor mats. I still went all in to be the best. That was non-negotiable for me. And it wasn't their fault that I hadn't run the numbers and realized I'd be taking a pay cut. That was on me, and it was a lesson well learned.

In August of 2004, during my second year at Eli Lily and six years after her diagnosis, my grandmother lost her life to Alzheimer's disease. It had been a long, slow decline that left my mother, our family, and me reeling with sadness for the vibrant woman we'd lost well before she passed away. The most difficult thing for me had been my helplessness to do anything to make her situation better in her final years. It reinforced in me that whatever I was doing for a living, my life must always be about service in some way.

———

While I worked at Eli Lily, I lived in the heart of Minneapolis, and my job left me plenty of time to enjoy the city. From the time I earned my first commission at Cintas, I'd been making the most of the single life, and I was still in it. I went out several nights a week with my friends, hitting the restaurants and bars or getting great seats for pro ball games. Most weekends, my boys and I were deep in the club, posted up in the VIP section, popping bottles and seeing who could pull the most women.

Part of our socializing included working out and playing ball at the practice facility for the Minnesota Timberwolves. When a couple of the women on the WNBA team asked me to play with them, I figured it would be fun. I went hard in the practice, blocking shots and playing to win. For me, it was all or nothing, and they appreciated that I didn't come in thinking I should take it easy on them.

One of the players invited me to come to one of their games, but in truth, I had zero interest in women's basketball. I went to the game just to be polite, but I left with a new respect for the way the WNBA played basketball at its best, below the rim, the way the game was originally meant to be played.

The WNBA players were also a part of our local social scene during that time. A lot of my crew hung out at a club right across from where the Timberwolves played, and so did they. One night, I noticed one of my homeboys talking to a tall, attractive woman, and my competitive instinct kicked in. We had an agreement that, unless she was your girl, any woman was fair game, so I pushed up and started my own conversation with her.

Her name was Tamika, and she and I had a lot in common, including a background in high-level sports. She had not only played basketball on the college level but had gone on to play in the WNBA. She lived in Columbus, Ohio, but we hit it off, and we saw each other when we could. In the coming months, I started to feel like it was time to end my phase of going out four or five nights a week and spending my time with one woman after another. My connection with Tamika was growing, and soon, we were in a long-distance relationship.

When I wasn't dating or hanging out, I filled the rest of my free time with volunteer opportunities. I mentored kids at local community centers, including the YMCA and the Boys & Girls Club. I reached out to kids from backgrounds similar to mine—young boys and girls who felt like they didn't fit in, young athletes who wanted to develop their skills, and teenagers looking for advice on how they could accomplish their educational and career goals. When a friend told me his sister's high school basketball team needed someone to help out, I decided to volunteer. It was a tough school, and I knew the students could use as many positive role models as possible. It was a great experience for me.

It seemed like the best of all worlds—a good job, a new relationship, and plenty of opportunities to give back to my community. And it was a good life, but once again, I felt the desire for a change. At Eli Lily, I had a job many people would envy, but I spent a lot of time in my car, and I didn't love driving. I serviced accounts in rural territories and out near the Mayo Clinic, which was over an hour away from where I lived. All of the driving started to wear on me, and once again, I imagined how different things might be if I had my own business.

I had always been a huge Michael Jordan fan, but I had also watched Magic Johnson as he developed his second career as a business owner after he retired from basketball. Few athletes of any caliber had created the kind of empire he was building. I especially admired the way he combined his profit-making enterprises with his mission to give back to under-served communities. I didn't personally know anyone who'd accomplished what Magic had in the business world, but I studied him from afar. I knew I could learn from his decisions, his habits, and his successes and failures.

Magic launched Magic Johnson Enterprises while he was still playing in the NBA. That kind of foresight was rare among athletes, and it impressed me. He invested in restaurants, health clubs, and even sports teams, but he also opened a movie theater and a Starbucks in neighborhoods that had been ignored by those kinds of businesses. He aligned with major corporations to market their products and services to new urban audiences.

His businesses improved the neighborhoods they were in and made the residents feel like their dollars counted as much as anyone else's. Magic's ventures provided jobs and career-growth opportunities that would otherwise have been unavailable for many of the people they employed. On top of all of that, he also created the Magic Johnson Foundation with a mission to "address the educational, health, and social needs of ethnically diverse, urban communities."

I studied Magic Johnson's entrepreneurial and philanthropic moves the same way I'd studied those videotapes of Michael Jordan's moves on the court when I was a kid. I still wasn't sure how I would get started or what line of business I wanted to be in. However, what I did know for sure was that building a business to line my pockets would never be enough. Of course, I wanted to afford the kind of lifestyle I'd dreamed of having for years. I wanted a nice car, a nice home, and the freedom to travel the world. But the success of any business I created would also be measured by how it impacted my team, my customers, and my community. The ultimate value would be measured in how I improved lives.

An acquaintance who ran a home mortgage company had talked to me about the potential to create wealth quickly in that industry. I decided to get my feet wet, and I liked the way the water felt. With my first couple of mortgages, I made a lot of money in a short amount of time. Finally, I decided to become a full-time mortgage broker agent. I was earning good money, and I was helping customers get low rates and quickly close on their home loans.

While I was very happy with the income I was earning, I also wanted to be smart and invest it for growth. After talking with my acquaintance and seeing his success in the business, I decided that real estate might prove to be the key to the kind of entrepreneurial freedom I was searching for. I planned to use some of that extra cash I earned from the mortgage business to redo the deck and the fencing on my own home, but I also decided to invest some of it in a rental property my mortgage-broker friend had for sale. It turned out to be a costly but valuable lesson in doing business.

———

The duplex I purchased promised to be a nice source of passive income, but it turned out to be anything but. The property was in a St. Paul community called Frogtown. It was in a crime-ridden neighborhood that attracted drug users and dealers and the kind of violence and other criminal activity that came with them. I didn't have a property management company, so I had to go knock on the door to collect the rent payments every month. I dreaded that chore. Sometimes, I'd bring a friend along to back me up or just be a witness to how things went down because, almost without fail, there was trouble when I showed up to collect the money my tenants owed me.

There was a high turnover rate among renters in the area, but when they fell behind on rent, eviction laws were on their side. From the tenants' point of view, it made sense that they couldn't be put out on the street in the middle of a Midwest winter, but as the landlord, it put me in a tough position. Those were months when I collected no rent at all, but I still had to pay the mortgage and expenses. On top of the trouble with tenants, I quickly discovered there were major problems with the property. Any money I collected had to go toward repairs, and soon after I bought it, my rental property was costing me more than it brought in.

At one point, I rented to a woman who worked as a stripper. Clearly, this was a bad idea, but she was willing to pay several months' rent upfront before she moved in, and I fell for the cash she flashed. One day, I stopped by the property, and my tenant had a proposal for me.

"You know, I also work as a masseuse. I can make more money if you let me run that business out of here."

"No," I told her. "You can't run any kind of business out of this property. It clearly says so in your lease." Given that she'd answered the door half dressed, I had a pretty good idea of what kinds of massages she was offering, and the last thing I needed was a prostitution ring operating out of my property.

After she'd gone through the rent she'd paid in advance, I stopped by to pick up her next month's rent payment. Again, she answered the door scantily dressed. She explained she didn't have the money, but she made it clear that she'd be willing to cover the rent by providing me with personal services.

That was the final straw for me. I served her and the man she had living with her with an eviction notice. She wasn't giving up that easily though. I was trying to have the house approved as a Section 8 rental property, which would mean the government subsidized the tenants' rent. That would have been good for me as an owner, since the government paid its portion reliably. However, this young lady knew how to work the system. To get back at me and slow down the eviction process, she called the housing authority and reported me for having rats and termites in the house.

None of that was true, but she succeeded in creating one more headache for me to deal with, and it bought her a little more time in the house. I had to make sure the property was ready for an unexpected inspection and deal with all of the back and forth with the agency. None of this was what I'd signed up for when I decided to become a landlord.

I felt like I was throwing money down a hole, and what was supposed to be a passive income source was taking up way too much of my time. I had to face the fact that I hadn't done my due diligence. I didn't properly inspect the property's condition before I agreed to buy it. Instead of crossing my Ts and dotting my Is on paper, I'd entered into the sale without a well-written contract to protect my interest.

The bottom line was that I'd relied on the trust I had for someone I called a friend rather than handling the transaction the way I should have. It was an expensive lesson, but it changed the way I functioned in the business world from that point on. I'd learned the importance of having a clear understanding and a signed contract with the proper protections for all parties in any business deal.

I'd had my first taste of entrepreneurship, and although it was bittersweet, I still wanted more—just not in real estate. Little did I know that an opportunity in an industry I'd always shied away from was just around the corner. But before I could get to that, I'd have to deal with major changes in my personal life—for better or worse.

CHAPTER THIRTEEN

He who is not courageous enough to take risks will
accomplish nothing in life. —Muhammad Ali

Early in 2005, I left the mortgage business and made the jump to Corporate Express. It was my third Fortune 500 employer, but I knew the job would only be temporary. I had never been clearer about the fact that I really didn't want to work for anybody else. I was determined to launch my own business, sooner rather than later. In the meantime, the job provided for my relocation to Columbus, Ohio, where Tamika, who still played in the WNBA, also worked as an assistant coach for Ohio State's women's basketball team.

The vision for my life that had begun to develop when I was a small child dreaming of the perfect family had matured into something richer and more substantial. I realized I had limitless opportunities, and whatever became of my life would be the result of my own decisions, not the byproduct of my parents' choices or my childhood experiences. Secondhand clothes and Section 8 housing were things of the past for me. I earned enough money to live in a nice place, take exotic vacations, and buy anything I wanted to wear. More importantly, I'd developed skills that would ensure I could always earn a good living.

My vision still included a stable family, and it looked like that would soon mean marriage. Tamika and I got along so well and accomplished so much that the people in our circle started to refer to us as the next "power couple." We both had the courage and ambition to go after big goals in our careers. It seemed like a perfect partnership. In October of 2006, after a couple of years of dating, I proposed to Tamika, and she accepted. Before long, wedding planning was underway.

In many ways, I was already living a dream come true, but the closer I got to marriage the clearer it became that there was a missing piece. In moments of clarity, I admitted to myself that I was still suppressing much of the anger, the sadness, and the disappointment of not knowing my father. It was all simmering just below the surface, kept at bay when I was younger by the screaming crowds, the trophies, the records I'd set, and the distraction of trying to keep my mother from self-destructing. As my life became more settled, I could no longer ignore my unresolved father issues.

I realized that I couldn't get married or start a family without doing everything in my power to solve the mystery of my father and the role he played, and failed to play, in making me the man I was. I couldn't be a husband, much less Dad to any child I might have in the future, until I'd done everything I could to sort through that part of my past. I had to do whatever I could to find my father and understand the part of my identity that was David Antoine Brumfield, his namesake.

My fiancée supported my decision to search for Slim and to try to find him before our wedding. I imagined having him there for the ceremony, introducing him to my friends, and seeing the pride in his eyes as his son took that big step, but I was also realistic. There were no guarantees that whatever my search turned up would make me happy at the end of the day.

It didn't make sense that I could miss a complete stranger, but I did miss him. Maybe it was a blood connection that ran through his veins and mine, or all the unanswered questions I'd been left with that day on the porch when I was seven years old, or maybe it was that no other man had ever been able to step in and completely fill the role of father for me. Whatever the reasons, I still felt the pain of his absence, and even though I knew I might fail, that possibility had never stopped me from going after what I wanted. I had to take a shot at finding my father.

One fall afternoon, only weeks after I'd gotten engaged, I sat alone in my living room. I opened my laptop and typed my father's name, David Henry Brumfield, into a search engine. What came up wasn't promising. There was a smattering of results with various spellings of his last name, but nothing I could run with. After an hour or two, I was no closer to locating my father than when I'd started.

When that didn't work, I tried a different strategy. Instead of searching for my father's name, I looked up different ways to find people. I came across a site that did background searches, and I started to feel hopeful. After all, everyone accumulates a record of addresses and phone numbers and other identifying information over the years. It may not be easily accessible to the public, but we all leave both a paper trail and a digital trail.

I typed in the information I had about my father, which wasn't much, paid the fee, and waited for the results. When the field for last known addresses came up populated, I froze. I was as scared as I was excited. Right there, in stark black and white, was a list of my father's previous addresses. In fact, the search results listed all of the addresses, emergency contacts, and phone numbers he'd given whenever he was arrested or picked up by the police for any reason.

I didn't recognize any of the names on the list of contacts, but there was no reason why I should have. My father was a stranger to me, and all of the people in his life, the women he'd been involved with and the friends who'd given him a place to crash now and again, were strangers to me too.

I couldn't believe how easy it had been. For the first time in my life, the possibility of finding my father seemed real. If I dialed one of the numbers on my computer screen, he might answer. He might be glad to hear from me. He might cry tears of joy and tell me he's been looking for me for years.

Or he might say he didn't want to have anything to do with me and hang up on me. There was always a chance that he'd turn his back on me if I reached out to him. Or even worse, someone else might answer at one of those phone numbers and tell me he was dead. It might be too late.

I considered slamming my laptop and forgetting the whole thing, but I'd come too far. I'd reached a bridge I had to cross if I was ever going to know what waited for me on the other side. So I dialed the first number and waited for a new chapter in my life to unfold.

———

The phone rang once, then twice, but I hung up before anyone could answer. My nervousness surprised me. I was closer than I'd ever been to finding the answers I'd wanted for most of my twenty-seven years, but I wasn't sure I was ready. I had to admit to myself for the first time that fear had been a big part of why I hadn't made more of an effort to find my father before that day.

I called a couple of numbers and got no answer. I called another, and a tone sounded to introduce a recording that told me, "The number you have reached has been disconnected." I let out a sigh of both relief and frustration.

With the phone gripped in my hand, I dialed the next number on my list. This time, a woman answered on the other end, but I hung up without saying a word to her. So many thoughts raced through my head. I needed to sort them out before I'd even know what to say.

I gave myself a minute, and then I took a deep breath, picked up the phone, dialed the number one last time, and waited for someone to answer. The same woman's voice said, "Hello?"

Before I could think, the words came pouring out of me, almost like I was making a cold call for a job. "Hello. My name is Benjamin Raymond. I was born David Brumfield. I'm calling because I'm trying to get in contact with my father, David Henry Brumfield, and this number was listed with his last known address."

"Who is this?" she asked.

"My name is Benjamin Raymond," I told her again. "It used to be David Antoine Brumfield, but my mother changed it when I was little. Do you know my father? I'm trying to find him, and this is one of the last known addresses for him. I haven't seen him or heard from him in twenty years."

I hoped she'd say, "Hold on. I'll get him for you." But there was silence on the other end of the line. I had no idea what this woman's relationship with my father might be. If she knew him at all, maybe he had hurt her. Maybe she wanted nothing more to do with him or his son. If his track record with my mother was any indication, then that was a distinct possibility.

The seconds ticked by, and I started to think making the call had been a mistake.

Finally, she explained that her name was Jane Roberts and my father had stayed with her a while ago. "You sound just like him," she said. "I might be able to help you. Why don't you give me your number? I'll see what I can do, and I'll call you back."

I rattled off my number twice to make sure she had it down.

"Give me a few days," she said, "and I'll see what I can find out for you."

I hung up the phone, not sure whether I had anything to celebrate yet or not. I had just spoken to a woman who knew my father and probably knew how to get in touch with him. I was so close.

———

For the next couple of days I could barely concentrate on my work or think about the wedding planning Tamika and I had taken on. In the middle of conversations, I'd lose track of what people were saying as my thoughts wandered to whether or not I'd hear my father's voice soon and how that conversation might go. I constantly checked my phone to make sure I hadn't missed a call from Ms. Roberts.

As one day stretched into the next, I wondered why it could possibly be taking so long for her to get back to me. Was she trying to hunt down my father because she hadn't seen or talked to him in years? Was she trying to convince him that he should call me because he really didn't want to be bothered? Had she given up altogether?

Just as I started to think I needed to reach out to her, Ms. Roberts called me back. It had only been a few days since we talked, but it felt like weeks. She explained that she'd met Slim through her boyfriend at the time.

"I wouldn't expect you to know this," she told me, "but Slim's in federal prison. He's been there since 2000 on drug charges. And he's still got a few years to serve."

"Okay," I said. I flashed back to all of the stories I'd heard about my father being a bad guy. Some part of me had known there was a chance I'd find him in prison, but I'd hoped for a better outcome.

"I talked to his caseworker there at the prison," Ms. Roberts told me. "Your father knows you're trying to reach him. And he really wants to talk to you."

"Okay," I said.

"So this is what they're going to do. Your father's caseworker will make sure your name is on the list. That way, he can call you, and you can visit him. I don't know if you can get out there—"

"Where's the prison?" I asked. It really didn't matter where it was. I'd travel any distance to finally lay eyes on my father again and have some of my questions answered.

"You have a pen? I'll give you all the information." Ms. Roberts explained that Slim was incarcerated in a federal prison in Pekin, Illinois. I couldn't call him or visit him until my name was added to the appropriate lists, but his caseworker was working to expedite my approval.

I did my best to thank her, but none of my words seemed like enough. She could have refused to get involved, but she'd gone to a lot of trouble for me, and I appreciated it more than I could say. After I hung up with Ms. Roberts, I slumped in a chair, overwhelmed with relief and anticipation. My father was in prison, but he wanted to see me just as much as I wanted to connect with him.

———

Slim had resided in the same prison for six years. After so much time, the prison staff knew him well, and they liked him. Apparently, his amiable personality served him well on the inside. He didn't cause trouble, and his good-natured attitude won him friends among the other inmates and officials. Because of their affinity for him and the way the story of his long-lost son finding him circulated, prison officials rushed through my approval. Not long after my conversation with Ms. Roberts, I got a call from my father.

Hearing his voice felt like a dream. I strained to pick up some familiarity in it, to see if I could recall it from the last time we'd talked, twenty years earlier. It did sound familiar, not because of my memories of that long-ago conversation but because Ms. Roberts had been right. My own voice sounded a lot like Slim's.

After so much time, I didn't know where to start, but my father dove right in. He told me all about his family, and I discovered I had four uncles, three still living, who I'd never known existed. As my father described his family to me—they were my family now too—I couldn't help thinking of what it would've been like to be raised surrounded by uncles who'd all grown up playing sports at school and with each other and who never let anyone come between them. The contrast between my father's upbringing in a two-parent household, with brothers who always had his back, and my solitary childhood, with no brothers or sisters and a mother who was only as present as her mania, delusions, and drug addiction would allow, was too remarkable to overlook.

My father explained that he'd lost his parents and his brother Ebb all within a span of one year. His father, William, who was born in 1900, passed away in 1988. Only six months later, my grandmother, Flora, died of a heart attack at seventy-seven. Finally, Ebb, the twin brother of Edward, died of leukemia just a few months later.

The Brumfields had suffered a lot of loss, but, my father said, their bond was still tight. I heard the pride in his voice when he shared that his oldest brother, William, owned a trucking company in Baton

Rouge, Louisiana. He gave me my uncle's phone number so I could connect with him too. I supposed my father wanted his older brother to be available to me in a way that my father couldn't until after he had served the rest of his sentence.

"You know," he said, "You also got a sister. She knows all about you."

I couldn't believe it. I had always wanted a brother or sister, but I was so used to being an only child that I'd never considered that I might already have siblings out there in the world, a brother or sister who I'd never met. As soon as my father said the words, it made sense. He'd been a young man when I was born, so it shouldn't have been surprising that, just as he went on to have other relationships after he and my mother broke up, he also had another child.

"I have a sister? What's her name?" I asked. "Where does she live? How old is she? She already knows about me?"

My father laughed. "Yeah, of course she knows about you. In fact, you probably don't remember this, but when you were a little boy, I came and saw you that one time. One of the reasons I was pushing so hard to get back in your life was because your sister was about to be born. I wanted you two to know each other, and my probation officer helped me find out where you and your mother were living." He told me my sister's name was Davida, and he gave me her number so I could get in contact with her.

My head spun. Although it was good news, it was almost more than I could process. I had focused single-mindedly on locating my father, but I'd also uncovered an entire family, from uncles and cousins to the fulfillment of one of my deepest wishes from early childhood, a sibling, a sister. I was over the moon with anticipation. I couldn't wait to talk to Davida.

———

The voice on the other end of the phone didn't sound like mine or my father's this time. My sister's voice was soft and shy, almost like she was uncertain about talking to me. I couldn't blame her. Even though my father had told her about me, he couldn't have shared much about the kind of person I was. He didn't know me any better than she did. She had no idea what she was getting into with her newfound brother.

This brother-sister relationship was a life-changing revelation for me, and I was anxious to get to know her. I felt confident that she was the answer to a prayer I'd all but given up on as a young boy. But Davida was in less of a rush. She already had three sisters and a brother on her mother's side, and she wasn't ready to leap into a family reunion with me just yet.

We talked a little about how and where we'd each grown up, and with just a few details from her life story, I could tell that she and I had a lot in common.

"Slim told me you have a daughter," I said.

"Yes," Davida told me, "Her name is Aniah."

I didn't want to overwhelm her, but over the next few weeks, we talked a few more times. Finally, I told Davida, "I want to come down to meet you and my niece."

Davida agreed. She may have been unsure about this new relationship, but I felt like a small part of the lifelong wound in my spirit had started to heal and it would heal even more when I could look my sister in the eye and give her a hug.

"I'll be there tomorrow," I told her. I had waited my whole life to connect with my father and his family, and once I knew she was open to meeting, I didn't want to wait a minute longer.

A snowstorm hit on the day I planned to drive from Columbus, Ohio, to Jackson, Tennessee, to visit my sister and some of her family, but I couldn't let that delay or deny me. The distance between the two cities was just over five hundred miles, and I set out to take the eight-hour journey on my own. I had given up road trips after taking more than my fair share of them in college and spending so much time on the road in sales, but I didn't want to waste time figuring out flights and rental cars. I just wanted to get there.

Six hours in, and I was still driving through a snowstorm. Traffic had been slow in places because visibility was bad, roads were slick, and drivers were too cautious to approach the speed limit. By the time I reached Nashville, with two hours left to drive, I could barely see where I was going. With little traffic on the highway, I could no longer rely on taillights in front of me to help me stay in my lane. Hours of driving in the blinding white was making me delirious.

The adrenaline that had fueled the first half of my drive began to wear off. I was exhausted, so I grabbed a cheap motel room just to close my eyes and get enough rest to be fresh enough to drive again. The roadside motel was one of those places that looked like it should charge by the hour. Inside my room, one wall was stained with something I hoped was splattered coffee. I decided not to turn on the light in the bathroom. Sometimes, I thought, it's better not to know.

I looked at the bed and tried not to imagine how long it had been since housekeeping had changed the sheets. I was so tired I had to take my chances. I wrapped my winter coat around me and lay on top of the covers. Every time I closed my eyes, the sound of a truck going by, pipes groaning, or another guest flushing a toilet kept me from drifting off. I tossed and turned for an hour, but it was useless. My body was worn out, but my mind was running at full speed. I was too pumped up to get any sleep. I got back on the road and headed out to meet my sister.

———

When I arrived at the family's duplex, I was disappointed to discover Davida wasn't there, but the rest of her family immediately embraced me and invited me in to wait for her. I got to know her sisters, her mother, and her nieces and nephews before I ever met my sister. But within an hour, Davida arrived, and I was face to face with my father's only other child.

Looking at Davida was like looking at a female version of myself. My sister also had a white mother, and we'd both ended up with the same tan complexion. We both had big, expressive eyes, and our father's full lips. If not for our age difference, we could've been twins. The experience was surreal for me, but it was new for Davida too. Her other brother and her sisters were all white, so it was her first time having a sibling who looked as much like her as I did.

My father had sent me photos from prison, and I could see that Davida and I both looked a lot like him. We were fair-skinned, where his complexion was a deep, rich brown, but our features were his. It was both thrilling and shocking. I'd spent a lifetime living in a family where not a single person looked like me, and now I could see myself in two different people.

I immediately fell for my three-year-old niece, Aniah. I was looking forward to becoming a father one day, and having a niece felt like good practice. I made a promise to myself that I would be a positive male role model for her as she grew up and protect and guide her as much as I could.

Davida was as quiet and reserved as she'd been on the phone, but she also had a loving, kind nature, and I felt protective of her as well. I only visited for a couple of days, but it didn't take long to break the ice between us. We hung out at some of her favorite local spots and tried to catch up on the two decades we'd missed of each other's lives.

Driving back to Columbus, I felt like I was flying. It had been one of the best experiences of my life, but there was a bigger moment yet to come. I still had to meet my father.

———

Two months after I met Davida in Tennessee, I flew into Chicago, picked up a rental car, and hit the freeway for the two-and-a-half hour drive to the prison where my father was incarcerated. Tamika had offered to come with me, but I felt like this was another leg of my journey that I had to travel alone. I couldn't fully articulate why at the time, but in looking back, I can see I compartmentalized my life. My father was my past, and I saw her as my future. I was still in the midst of trying to understand who I was as a black man raised without a single black role model in my daily life. Meeting my father would be essential to figuring out my own identity, but the thoughts and emotions that ran through my head and my heart raced in every possible direction.

He knew I was on the way, and I hoped he was as eager to lay eyes on me as I was to finally see him again. As I drove through the winter-barren landscape, a soundtrack of hip hop and gospel filled the car. It was much of the same music I'd listened to before games in my senior year of high school. I was a hip hop fan through and through, but my playlist also included some gospel music that touched my spirit in a different way. High school had been such a tumultuous time, and Kirk Franklin's *Nu Nation Project* album had given me hope when I needed it most.

Two songs in particular carried me through the loneliness and despair that hit me when I worried about my mother or wondered why my life continued to be so unstable. "Lean on Me," a song that promised we'd always have someone to turn to, and "Blessing in the Storm," with its message that out of all the bad, some good would come, had provided me just a little of the comfort I needed back then. As I listened to the lyrics so many years later, I saw myself as a kid again. I flashed back on all the highs and lows I'd gone through, and in each image, there was a gaping void where Slim should have stood beside me.

When I won my first soccer game and when my mother was hospitalized for weeks at a time, where was my father?

When I was starting on the varsity basketball team as a freshman and when my mother was deep in her drug addiction and under the control of her abusive boyfriend, where was my father?

When I was voted homecoming king and when I moved from the Schades to the Nesbitts back to the Schades and finally to live with the Hughes family, where was my father?

When I took the court to play in front of 20,000 fans and when I needed a few dollars just to put gas in my car to get to work, where was David Henry Brumfield?

I saw myself as a scared little boy, waiting for my mother to come home and wondering if she'd be beaten and bruised when she finally did. I saw myself as a teenager, and even though I had all of the popularity and accolades that seemed like a teenager's dream come true, I was still a lonely kid who wanted reassurance that I would still be loved if I never picked up another football or basketball again.

I went back to when my mother was newly married, and I saw her and Derrel throwing their lives away behind their addictions. I saw the Hughes family open their home and their hearts to me. I was back with Mom Kat as she listened to me and talked with me in a way that few people ever had. I went back to Hugh, who held me to the same standards he held his own sons to, giving me a taste of the kind of fatherly tough love I'd never had from my own father.

I let the same songs play over and over, the words taking on new meaning for me now that I was a grown man and especially as I tried to sort through the anger, the resentment, the love, the excitement, the fear, and the anxiety all bubbling up in me as I barreled south on I-55, heading toward my father, who, for me, represented both my history and my destiny.

How, I wondered, would my life have been different if he'd been around for even a few of those significant moments in my life? What was so important that it would keep him away from me even when he wasn't doing time? How could he choose drugs and a life of crime over the chance to be involved in his only son's life?

I had two hours and thirty minutes to figure out exactly what I'd say when I looked my father in the eye. The drive was over before I knew it, and perhaps, just a bit before I was ready.

––––––––

The Federal Correctional Institution, Pekin, was a medium-security prison for male inmates. It housed up to twelve hundred inmates at any one time. Built in 1994, it was a relatively new facility that included a smaller minimum-security building, which, at the time my father was there, housed female inmates. The men my father lived among were convicted of crimes ranging from racketeering, conspiracy, and drug trafficking to bank robbery, extortion, money laundering, and the most violent of offenses. Pekin was famously known as the permanent home of Joseph Miedzianowski, a lifer known as the most corrupt police officer in Chicago history. Every day, my father navigated a population that included rapists, gang-bangers, and murderers.

Federal prisons are designed to intimidate, and Pekin didn't disappoint. For starters, it was built in the middle of nowhere. If a prisoner should manage to escape, he'd have nowhere but open fields to run to for miles. From a distance, the prison's campus looked like a fortress surrounded by barbed wire fencing and sprawling green lawns. A United States flag whipped and snapped in the brisk February wind. As I drove up to the main building and followed the signs for visitor parking, I was nearly giddy with excitement, but at the same time, I was really afraid.

Somehow, it was both the happiest and scariest moment I'd experienced in my twenty-eight years on earth. No game-winning shot or devastating loss on the court could have stirred up the mix of emotions inside of me at that moment. From my earliest memory, I'd wanted to have my father in my life. He was locked behind prison walls, but we were finally going to be reunited.

Three years earlier, I'd imagined this moment when I'd gone to see the movie *Antwone Fisher*. Sitting in the theater, watching a young black man embark on a journey to find his family and uncover his true identity, I felt like I was watching my own story play out on the big screen. The details of the screenwriter's life were different from my life story, of course, but the loss of identity, the profound loneliness, the primal need to connect with the man who brought him into this world, the pain of being abandoned and neglected, and the struggle to figure out why he'd been born into such circumstances were desires and emotions I understood all too well.

Sports had given me an outlet for the anger, pain, and sadness I didn't know how to express as a boy or as a young man. Fisher's character, on the other hand, never had that kind of escape from the harsh reality he grew up in, and he entered manhood defensive, angry, and always ready for a fight. Watching the story unfold, it was so clear to me that, without the discipline and confidence I got from athletics and the support of the families who took me in when I needed it most, my life could have gone down a very different path.

I left the theater that day emotionally drained from reliving my own journey while I rooted for Fisher to find what he needed in his search for his family. I also left more determined than ever to connect with the side of my family I'd never known. I needed to understand that history and find my place in it.

In that moment, I was ready to find my father and have a man-to-man conversation with him about where he'd been and why he'd never come back for me. But life had gotten in the way. Right about that time, my mother and Derrel's drug use put them in a bad situation, and the two of them went through one crisis after another. It took all of my time and energy to fight for my mother's well-being, and it was a battle I almost lost when things got so bad that I considered cutting her out of my life. I'd pushed my father out of my mind to focus on what seemed most urgent at that moment.

While some people might see the years that had passed since then as wasted, I'd come to see it as God's perfect timing. I needed to reach this point in my life before I reconnected with Slim. I needed to mature, grow past some of my anger and resentment, and become more open and curious. And now the time had come.

I pulled into a space in the prison parking lot and turned off the car's engine. Just on the other side of that wall, the father I'd been trying to find all of my life waited for me.

CHAPTER FOURTEEN

Forgiveness is the foundation for healing.

Visiting an inmate in prison is an involved process. You can't just decide one day that you want to go see someone you know who happens to be incarcerated. The prisoner has to apply to have your name added to his approved visitors list before you can even think of showing up to see him. He fills out part of the application, and then it's sent to you to fill in your part. It helps if you're family because only a limited number of non-relatives are allowed to visit any one prisoner. If there's any question about your suitability, prison officials will run a thorough background check on you, and they can deny your application if they find you have your own criminal history or associations.

What many people don't realize is that the average federal prisoner is incarcerated five hundred miles from his or her home. Depending on your perspective, that might sound like a fair consequence for some of the crimes they've committed, but it's easy to forget that everyone who loves that prisoner gets the same sentence he gets. His wife or girlfriend, son or daughter, parents, siblings, aunts and uncles, and friends now have to make a decision. They either have to figure out a way to make a one-thousand-mile round trip, seven hours of driving time each way, or live without seeing their loved one until his sentence is served. Many families choose the latter because the travel is simply a burden they can't bear.

Once you've been approved to visit and have figured out how you'll get to the institution, you have to plan your schedule around the visiting hours, which are limited to two or three days a week. You may only see your loved one during the designated hours and for the maximum allotted time.

When you dress for the visit, choose your wardrobe carefully. Don't wear anything too short, tight, or revealing. Tank tops, hats, headbands, and military style clothing are forbidden. So are shorts that stop above the knees, graphic tees with words or images that might be considered offensive or provocative. Avoid any colors or attire that might make you look like you're affiliated with a gang. Stay away from anything that could make you look like you belonged in a cell. In the case of Pekin, that means avoiding khaki clothes since the prisoners wear work boots and khaki uniforms.

Besides your ID, car keys, and up to twenty dollars in cash, almost anything else you've brought with you has to be left in the car. Cell phones and cameras of all kinds are banned. There's no bringing in gifts, books, magazines, photos, or food from the outside. At best, you can treat your loved one to a snack from the vending machines in the visiting room, which you may use but he may not. Parents can bring in the basic necessities to care for a baby they've brought on the visit, but all personal items need to be carried in a clear plastic bag.

Inside, you are allowed to share one hug, kiss, or handshake with the inmate, "within the bounds of good taste," at the start of the visit.

Corrections officers monitor the public displays of affection to make sure they're not too long or too intimate and to ensure that visitors and inmates aren't passing contraband between them.

Each prisoner may have no more than seven visitors at one time. Visits may be cut short if the inmate doesn't arrive early enough, if there are too many people waiting for visits, or if the Visiting Room Officer decides to cut them short for any other reason. At the end of the visit, you may give your loved one another brief hug, kiss, or handshake as you say goodbye.

I was fortunate that traveling to the prison wasn't a problem for me. If I'd found my father years earlier, it would've been a struggle, but I could easily afford a flight and a rental car to get out to the facility, making me one of the lucky ones. I'd done everything I could to get ready for the visit and stay on the right side of the rules, but nothing could have really prepared me for the feeling of entering a medium-security federal prison.

There was no question that I had arrived at a correctional facility. Security vehicles patrolled the parking lot. Staring up at the walls I spied guards with guns, ready to pick off any threat from inside or outside of the fence. When I was instructed to, I popped the trunk of my rental car so guards could inspect it for contraband, weapons, or other prohibited items. I was relieved when they didn't search the rest of the vehicle. I had nothing to hide, but I had waited long enough to meet my father.

———

I parked alongside the other visitors, took my license and a couple of tens out of my wallet and dropped them in a plastic baggie, and I got out of the car. At the first security station, I showed my ID and went through the metal detectors. At the next station, I handed over my ID again, and I gave Slim's name and prisoner number.

"Wait here," the guard said. As I was about to discover, my day would be filled with more of the same—wait here, wait there, wait.

I stood outside the steel double doors until I was buzzed in. As I stepped through the doorway, the doors closed behind me, and I stood facing another set of thick double doors. Essentially, I was trapped in that little vestibule until someone let me out. It was an eerie feeling, almost like they could keep me there forever if they really wanted to, like they could take my freedom at any time.

When I was buzzed through the second set of doors, I stepped into a wide room filled with neatly organized tables and chairs. Several inmates, dressed in khaki uniforms, were already meeting with their visitors, and I checked out the wild mix of characters as I approached the attendant. Again, I gave Slim's name and number.

"Table number fourteen," he told me. "Not the yellow chair, that's for the inmates. Wait there. We'll call him."

I felt some of the inmates looking me up and down as I took a seat and glanced around at my father's community. At the table to my left, a white man with tattoos covering every exposed part of his body, including his face and his bald head, sat with a young man and woman. To my right, three generations of women visited with a middle-aged black man.

Every time I heard the prisoner's entry door buzz, I looked up, expecting to see my father walk through the doorway, but the minutes passed and Slim didn't appear. After more than half an hour had gone by, I started to worry that I'd come all that way for nothing. I went back to the Visiting Room Officer and asked him if there was any word on my father.

The officer frowned. "He should've been here by now. We called him when you came in. Don't worry about it. I'll call him again."

I went back to my table. I could feel the tension in the room. While some of the visitors sat and talked with inmates like they were having Saturday afternoon lunch at the mall food court, others sat with their arms folded and mouths clamped shut, giving the occasional one-word answer. Little children laughed and fought for their fathers' attention. Teenagers sulked, and as their fathers tried to give them advice, they nodded, but they looked at him with eyes that said, "You might be my dad, but you ain't shit." I could relate to it all.

After another twenty minutes, the buzzer sounded again, and the prisoner's entry door swung open. I broke into a huge smile as my father smiled back at me and came into the visiting room. I stood up to hug him before he took his seat at our table. As my father put his arms around me, I realized the moment was real. It wasn't a dream or a wish. I was actually standing face to face with the man who I'd spent my life wondering about, searching for, and longing to know. I could reach out and touch the man who had given me life but left me to figure out my own identity and find my own place in the world.

"You had me out here waiting so long I started to think you weren't coming," I told my father. "What took you so long?"

Slim laughed. "I never heard them call me. I was in the barbershop. Wanted to get a fresh cut before our visit."

I chuckled to myself. I had done the same thing before I left home. Like father like son.

"Everybody knows you're coming today," my father told me. "They're excited about me finally meeting my son."

We engaged in a little small talk, and I asked Slim about some of the other inmates in the room, what they were in for and whether he ever had any trouble with any of them. I was curious about what his life was like inside.

"We work," my father told me. "I work in the kitchen, doing whatever needs to be done. We can make a little money to spend in here."

Our time was limited, and I didn't want to leave without getting to the questions I'd waited more than twenty years to ask. "So what happened?" I asked my father. "Why'd you just disappear like that?"

"Your mother and her family did not want me around, son. I was always trying to see you, but they wouldn't let me anywhere near you."

No matter how many ways I asked the question, Slim's answer was the same. *He had tried*, but people got in the way. *He had tried*, but then he got locked up. *He had tried*, but he lived too far away. *He had tried*, but he couldn't find me. *He had tried*, but he got locked up again. *He had tried*!

When our visit came to an end, I promised my father I'd be back to see him. As I made the long drive back to Chicago, I realized I wasn't really satisfied with any of my father's excuses. I thought I had forgiven him for disappearing from my life, but I felt some of the old resentment well up. I had spent years believing I needed my father in my life, but now that I had found him, I was starting to realize that wasn't true. I wanted him in my life, but maybe I'd never really needed him at all.

———

Back at home, Tamika and I were still in the wedding planning process, and I was trying to decide what my next career move would be. In the midst of all this, I was anxious to build a relationship with my sister. She still wasn't as excited as I was, but I was determined to do what I could to solidify our status as brother and sister.

One month after my first visit with Slim, I flew to Indianapolis for the Big 10 Tournament. My sister, Davida, and my niece, Aniah, flew in to meet me in Indy, and together, we traveled back to Pekin to visit my father as a family. As overwhelmed with emotions as I'd been on my first trip, the second time around was even more dramatic, and in many ways, more stressful.

This time, there were so many more family dynamics going on between the four of us. Even little Aniah, who was just three years old, had mixed feelings. On some level, she must have been aware of the range of feelings her mother went through during our visit, but she also had her own thoughts and feelings about her grandfather. They talked over the phone whenever Slim and Davida talked, and as much as you could love someone you'd never met in person, Aniah loved her grandfather. This was her first time laying eyes on the man behind the voice.

There's a certain amount of innocence lost when children visit their loved ones in prison. The world becomes a scarier, more confusing place for them, but for many children like Aniah, the only alternative is to never get a chance to hug their grandfather or grandmother, mother or father, or whoever has the sentence. Over the years, as she grew older, my sweet little niece would have to sort through what the experience meant for her. It had to have a lasting impact, but I was determined to do what I could to make sure Slim's life was a cautionary tale for her, not a model for the kind of man she should be with or the kind of life she should lead.

Because I wasn't yet a parent, I could only imagine how Davida felt knowing that her precious daughter was sharing a room with convicted murderers, rapists, and child molesters. Even though we hadn't known each other long, I felt incredibly protective of my sister and my niece in that environment. Davida must have felt some resentment about having to bring her child into that space. Slim wasn't some wrongfully convicted man fighting to have his sentence overturned. His own bad choices had landed him back behind bars. Davida had watched him lose his freedom and leave her life because of decisions he made.

Unlike me, Davida had grown up with Slim around. His relationship with her mother had lasted for years, but it was a complicated one. The two broke up while Davida was still a young child, but it was clear to everyone in the family that Davida's mother harbored a certain amount of fear of Slim. According to other family members, Slim had been violent with her, just as he had with my mother and other women in his life. While she maintained contact with him because of his relationships with Davida and Davida's older siblings, she also kept her distance.

Davida brought all of that family baggage with her on our visit. Even though she talked to him regularly by phone, she hadn't looked him in the eye since he was incarcerated seven years earlier. I could see conflicting emotions tugging at her. On the one hand, she was angry and hurt. On the other hand, in her heart, she was still a daddy's girl. It was a tough position for her to be in.

As they talked, Slim would periodically ask Davida to do him a favor on the outside. Call this person or that person, or put money on his books. Each time he asked her to do one more thing, I saw Davida shut down a little bit more. I wished he could see that she just wanted to be his daughter, not his errand girl on the outside and certainly not his provider.

We happened to be visiting on one of the prison's monthly family photo days, and we took our first family portrait, the first picture I was ever in with my father. It was just a shame that, in a lasting memory of our first time all together, surrounded by the people closest to him in this world, Slim was wearing prison khakis.

Leaving at the end of our visit was hard on both Davida and Aniah. Slim had been in good spirits. He looked healthy, he was working his kitchen job, and he was talking about his walk with the Lord. It wasn't like we'd found him beaten down or barely making it. He had been there long enough to know the ropes, and with so much structure and oversight, he stayed out of trouble. He knew how to work the system.

It would have been devastating to discover that he was fighting for his life every day, so we were all glad to find him well. Still, when we left, Davida and Aniah had no idea if they'd ever see Slim again before he finished his sentence. Aniah's little shoulders dropped with disappointment when we told her it was time to go. She didn't understand why her grandfather couldn't leave with us. Like so many of the children leaving that day, she broke down in tears. We all shared a final round of hugs, and our short moment as a family came to an end.

———

In April, Tamika and I were married in front of more than one hundred fifty of our family and friends. It snowed on our wedding day, an unusual occurrence for that time of year in Columbus, Ohio, but everything went off as planned, and we celebrated our union with a big formal wedding. Having my sister and some of Slim's family at the wedding meant a lot to me, but it still hurt that, even after we'd reunited, my father was missing one more of my major life events.

When I look back, it's amazing how little I knew what about what it meant to be married. In my entire life, I'd never seen my mother in a healthy relationship with a man. Instead, I'd watched her deal with men who came with drug abuse, black eyes, and calls to the police. I'd never seen my father in a relationship at all, but from what I'd learned of him over the years, it was pretty clear that he'd been violent and unfaithful with my mother and the other women in his life.

Based on my parents' examples, I knew what I didn't want in a relationship. However, I didn't realize how important it was for the two of us to come together and clearly define what kind of marriage we wanted to have. We were fairly young to be getting married, not even thirty years old yet, and we were both at crucial crossroads in our careers. Those two factors would have made the newlywed years difficult enough, but I was also still at the very beginning of understanding who I was as I got to know my father better, and a turn of events that would separate my wife and I was on the horizon.

I didn't understand the essence of marriage or the importance of laying a solid foundation for the relationship ahead of all other things. I thought I was ready. I thought we could handle all of these major changes, and more to come, while we built a marriage. But as it would turn out, I was wrong.

CHAPTER FIFTEEN

Faith doesn't make it easy.
Faith makes it possible.

I wasn't the only member of my family who made the move to Columbus. Shortly before my wedding, my mother had called me, and over the phone, her voice sounded more desperate than I had ever heard it. She skipped the small talk and spoke quietly and deliberately. "We're going to die, Ben," she said.

The pronouncement came out of nowhere. In all of my mother's delusional states and depressions, she had never said those words, and I didn't know what to think. I pressed her to explain what she meant by such a dire prediction.

"We're going to die here," she said again. "We're in it so bad."

By "we," she meant Derrel and her, and by "it," she meant the drugs. Derrel still had an addiction to crack. My mother had her own addiction on top of her mental illness and her inconsistent use of her prescribed medications. Together, they had gone through cycles of use and sobriety over the years, and together, they'd had times when they were lost to it all—running scams, breaking the law, and doing whatever it took to get the next high—but they had always bounced back. This time was different. My mother was calling me to help pull them back from the edge.

As much as she'd frustrated me over the years, I still loved this woman with my whole heart, and I knew a lot of the good in me had come from her. She may have dropped the ball with me at different points in my life, but when she was on her game, she gave me everything she could. I wasn't going to dismiss or underestimate her plea for someone to rescue her.

Saving my mother also meant saving her husband. Once he'd served his sentence for the check-cashing scam the two of them had been arrested for, he and my mother had moved to Beaver Dam. They'd lived there ever since, and while he'd managed to stay out of jail, Derrel hadn't stayed out of trouble. Aunt Bonnie had given him the opportunity to manage some property for her, and it hadn't gone well. Derrel was supposed to take care of odd jobs, like painting and small repairs, but she also put him in charge of collecting the rents. Much of that money never made it to my aunt's hands.

It would be easy to say that Aunt Bonnie should have known better than to let an addict have access to her funds, but Derrel could be quite convincing. He had burned bridges all over their small town, and now they had no one to turn to for a loan or any kind of assistance. Although his behavior frustrated me, I also had a grudging, growing respect for Derrel, and I didn't want to see him come to harm either. Yes, he was an addict, and he and my mother definitely used together, but he had also stuck by her for a decade, a lot longer than anyone else had. No one knew better than I did how trying it could be to live with her when she was manic or depressed. Yet Derrel never abandoned her. They were so tight through it all that I started calling them Bonnie and Clyde.

It was a struggle for me to try and see the good in Derrel, when their situation had deteriorated so far. I remembered the times when I'd come home from college and find their refrigerator empty because they'd spent all of their money on crack. But I also thought back on the times when he'd come to my games or gone to open gyms with me and the times when he'd made me laugh.

Once, he'd offered to drop me at the airport so he could grandstand in the Corvette he'd recently bought. I threw my bag in the back, and the two of us folded our more than six-foot-tall bodies into his two-seater for the ride to the terminal. After I dragged myself out of the car, I turned to wave goodbye. Derrel wanted to show off the power of his engine, and he revved it a couple of times and then tried to take off like someone had just waved the flag at NASCAR. Unfortunately, he had his foot on the brake and the gas at the same time. The car lurched forward into traffic. The airport was crowded, and by the time he got up to speed, he had to slam on the brake. I laughed as I walked into the terminal. That was just Derrel—always trying to impress, but never quite pulling it off.

I hadn't lived in the same city as my mother and stepfather for several years, and I had to admit I was leery of getting too involved in their situation. However, in that moment, I had to make a decision. I could try to pacify my mother with money or help from a distance and hope for the best, or I could do everything in my power to assist her and her husband in climbing out of the deep, dark hole they'd dug for themselves. There was only one choice I could make.

"You're not going to die, Mom," I told her. "Go get Derrel, and this is what I want you to do. Listen to me now."

"I'm listening," my mother said.

"I want you two to pack everything you can fit in the car and just drive straight here to Columbus. It's gonna be okay. I'll have everything ready for you. But you need to leave now."

As soon as I hung up the phone, I got to work. I leased a one-bedroom apartment for my mother and her husband in a decent neighborhood. If they were that deep into drugs, then they would have very little money, so I furnished the apartment with the basics and stocked their pantry and fridge. I didn't want them to have any reason to feel like they couldn't make it in Columbus. Later, I would find out I was right about the money. They had burned through over fifty thousand dollars of my mother's trust fund, and they had nothing to show for it.

While I was handling things on my end, they loaded everything they had into the two old cars they owned, and made their way from Beaver Dam to Columbus. I welcomed them to their new home, but they were adults and they'd have to decide for themselves whether they would use this new beginning to get their lives back on track or not. I prayed they would, but I had done my part.

The eight-hour driving distance from their drug-using social circle and the space to start over fresh proved to be exactly what they both needed. The next year of my mother's life would be one of the best she'd had in a very long time. She enjoyed living in a college town, and the small city size made her feel comfortable driving herself, a chore she usually avoided out of nervousness. She and Derrel settled into a relatively normal life for a while.

I was proud of the way my mother made the transition, but the cycle of drug abuse and descent into mental illness didn't disappear with the move. They both struggled with issues they'd never managed to deal with and move on from, and they would periodically return to drugs to dull the pain. My mother had never found a way to constructively deal with her mental illness and the dreams it had cost her, her childhood trauma, the rape she'd never recovered from, her guilt about the way I'd been raised, and a host of other issues that could send her spiraling down into depression.

As for Derrel, he carried with him through life a lot of sadness and regret over his lack of a relationship with his own son. He also felt bitter and resentful because he had once been an exceptional athlete with the potential to play in the Majors. He'd made it to the Minor League, but he never got the opportunity to find out how far he could go. I'm sure he'd left a lot of other broken dreams along the way too. He and I had our conflicts over the years, and we would have more, but I recognized a decent guy beneath all the issues, and I deeply appreciated his loyalty to my mother.

Their move to Columbus changed the dynamic between the three of us. One day, my mother and Derrel had a falling out, and he threatened to leave her and drive back to Milwaukee. A little distance might have been just the thing they needed at that moment, but he wanted to take their car, and he wanted the title. To me, that was a clear sign that he planned to sell the vehicle, and I could imagine how fast he'd go through the money. The car belonged to my mother, and I refused to hand over the title.

Before long, the two of us were in each other's faces and someone called the police.

"This is our car!" Derrel told the police. "I want the title."

While Derrel sputtered with anger, I remained calm. "Sir," I said. "I am the trustee for my mother. He can go, but the title remains because if I need to repo it, I will."

"That's my wife, and I want our car!" Derrel yelled.

"Officer," I said, "who are you going to believe?"

When all was said and done, I prevailed, but my mother was devastated by seeing the two men she loved the most go at each other like that. "Ben, you know I love Derrel. And I love you. I need you to find a way to get along."

She was right. I made a decision from that day that I'd handle Derrel differently for her sake. I had to give up the idea that I should have any say-so in who my mother chose to spend her life with. I determined to shift the way I looked at my stepfather, focusing on the things I liked about him and emphasizing them over his short-comings. Just as I'd learned to love and accept my mother with all of her failings, I chose to do the same for her husband.

————

With my mother settled and safe and the wedding behind Tamika and me, I was more determined than ever to get my own entrepre-neurial venture up and running. I could see all of the options that lay out before me, but as far as I was concerned, insurance wasn't one of them. To a young, high-energy, ambitious guy like me, it had always seemed like one of the most boring, stodgy industries in the world of business. Hugh had built a successful career in insurance, but whenever he tried to point me in that direction, I waved him off. That was an old man's game, and I had zero interest in it. I wanted to do something more exciting.

As I tried to figure out what kind of business I wanted to go into, Tamika suggested I meet her friend Al Sicard. During his time at the University of Dayton, Al had been named a McDonald's All-American and was nominated for the Converse All-American team. He was also deeply involved in community service, and I could tell he and I would speak the same language before we even met. Al was about a decade ahead of me in his career, and like Hugh, his business was insurance.

One of my strengths in sports had always been my willingness and ability to observe what others did well and learn from it. I had no problem asking questions to figure out how to get better at my game. In my drive to achieve greatness, I had no problem humbling myself to learn from those who had already gotten there, and that same curiosity had served me well in business. I really didn't want to hear about insurance, not from Hugh and not from Al, but I was confident I could learn something from him about entrepreneurship. At worst, I figured we'd at least have sports to talk about.

When we finally got together, Al asked if I was interested in insurance, and I had to tell the truth. He didn't try to debate me on the issue. Instead, he reached into a desk drawer, pulled out a check, and handed it to me.

"So what's that for?" I asked. "Last quarter?"

"That's what I made in the last fifteen days," Al said.

He had my attention.

————

After my talk with Al, I did a complete turnaround on the insurance business. Al helped me see that it wasn't the scam I sometimes thought it was. It was a way of helping people protect themselves, their families, and their property. It could mean the difference between the death of a loved one leaving a family in poverty and leaving them with the resources they need to pay the bills and still have time to grieve.

I soon discovered there were almost limitless ways insurance and the related financial services could be used to help clients move up in life. It was just the kind of business I was looking for, one that would allow me to be of service while I created prosperity for my family and myself.

I was happy to put myself under Al's tutelage. We had a lot in common, and as we worked together, Al and I would develop a strong friendship. He helped many people, including me, to open agencies, and his commitment to reaching back to make sure other people got a chance to have that kind of opportunity would inspire me to do the same in coming years. I was fortunate to have Al share his wisdom and advice with me at the start of my journey. I continued to work my full-time job, and after work, I'd take the hour-long drive to Dayton to learn from him. I decided I wanted to go after my own agency, and I decided to target one of the biggest insurance companies in the nation. I decided to go after an agency in Ohio. It wasn't my first choice of a place to live, but Tamika still had her coaching job there.

The process to become an agency owner is intense and time-consuming. It requires a lot of study and testing, with multiple interviews along the way, and a demonstration of preparedness. No matter how smart you are, how much money you have, or how eager you are to become an entrepreneur, you cannot skip a step. This is a time when the ability to focus on a long-term goal will serve you well. You cannot rush the process. Here's what it looked like at the time I went through it.

Step 1: Take a detailed assessment designed to test your knowledge of the insurance business and your leadership ability and gather information about your employment background and financial situation. If you don't receive an acceptable score, you must wait at least one year before taking the assessment again.

Step 2: Sit for the next assessment. This one dives more deeply into your knowledge, experience and abilities to determine your probability of success as an agency owner. Again, if you don't receive an acceptable score, you must wait at least one year before retesting.

Step 3: Submit yourself to a thorough background check that includes review of work history, education, driving record, and existing criminal record, and credit history. If you do not pass the background check, you cannot move on to the next step.

Step 4: Complete a series of training modules designed to give you a full view of the responsibilities, duties, and daily activities of an agency owner. Demonstration of your understanding of the module materials is required to move on to the next step.

Step 5: Bring to bear all of the knowledge you've picked up through the process to create and present a detailed business proposal that can stand up to the scrutiny of a panel of decision-makers. A successful presentation is required to move on to the next step.

Step 6: Choose an agency opportunity for which you want to compete. This part of the process is contingent upon confirmation that you have received the appropriate state licenses. Proper licensing and company approval are required to move on to the next step.

Step 7: Interview with the leadership in your region of interest. If you are chosen among all applicants to move forward, you must still have a clean background check and drug test to move on to the next step.

Step 8: Congratulations! If you've reached this step, you are now officially an employee of the company. During the four-month agency-owner training period, you will receive hands-on experience and in-depth training with company-specific products, policies, and procedures. Successful completion of this training period is required to receive an offer to become an independent agent, or agency owner, for the company.

Step 9: Did you think you were done? Not quite. You must still earn your contract with the company by reaching the goals set for you as an owner.

In a process that lasted several months, I went all-out to earn that agency opportunity. I made it all the way through seven of those eight steps. I went into the final round confident that I had given my best effort and expecting the win. In the end, it came down to two candidates, a woman and me. And the company chose to give the agency to her.

Nowhere along the way had I seen her demonstrate that she was more qualified than I was, so the decision threw me for a loop. Of course, I didn't know everything about how my competition had performed during the application process, but I did know how well I'd prepared myself. I had put in the work, and when I didn't get the agency, I felt like the athlete everyone expects to get picked in the first round of the draft but who drops down to the third.

I had never liked losing, and this loss felt like a big one. It left me with something to prove to the company and to myself. I'd learned over the years that the best way to recover from a setback was to get back in the game. I could have gone after another opportunity in Ohio, but I decided to raise the bar and consider an agency in a major city, where the competition would be tougher but the rewards could be even greater, and I found an opportunity to pursue in Dallas, Texas, one of the most lucrative regions for the insurance industry.

Dallas was such a tough market that several people warned me that I needed to think smaller. Even Al, who had inspired me to go into insurance in the first place, called me to try to convince me to change my mind. "You already failed at the high school level," he said, referring to the Ohio agency, "and now you want to play in the big leagues!"

I hung up on him. He had my best interest at heart, but there was something Al didn't know about me yet. Once I made a decision, I could tune out all of my doubters and focus on reaching my goal. I'd done it so many times before in sports and in life, and I was determined to do it again. I was going to prove the naysayers wrong. I was going to land that agency, and I was taking it to number one.

I went through the entire process again, this time flying back and forth to Dallas for interview after interview. As it came down to the wire, I pulled an all-nighter at Kinko's to prepare for the final approval process. I wanted everything as close to perfect as possible. I left no loose ends and no reasons to deny me. And in the end, I won the agency. In November of 2007, seven months after I started my life as a married man, I was hired by the company. It was a big accomplishment, but the process wasn't over. I still had to secure the required licenses.

I needed to get those licenses before the end of year, which meant the holiday season was really test-prep season for me. Studying for my Series 6 and 63 exams was an experience in itself. It was the most intensive study I'd ever had to do. These exams are required in order to legally sell certain financial products. For the Series 6, you get a maximum of two hours and fifteen minutes to complete one hundred multiple-choice questions. A score of seventy percent or higher is considered passing. For the Series 63, you're given one hour and fifteen minutes to answer sixty multiple-choice questions. You must score seventy-two percent or higher to pass.

Candidates pay big money for prep courses to prepare for these important exams. There's a lot of information to cover and a lot at stake for each test-taker. You can't launch an agency without passing. That's why, when my score popped up on the computer monitor and I saw that I had failed the first test, I couldn't believe it.

I'd never claimed to be the best student, but when I failed by a single point, I could only be mad at myself. In the past, I'd been able to rely on my skills as a salesperson and the force of my personality to get what I wanted in business. This was the first time those assets couldn't help me at all. You either passed the test or you didn't—and I hadn't. I had to admit that I could have been more focused in my studying, but I couldn't allow one point to stand in the way of my dream. You get three chances to pass these tests, and after that, you're out of luck. I wasn't going to blow it again, and there was no way I'd quit so close to the finish line.

After that first attempt, I went into pass-or-die mode. I stopped shaving and let my beard grow out. I wore sweatpants every day and went to Starbucks to study, downing lattes to stay focused and awake. When the words ran together on the page or I started to nod, I'd stand up and study. During that time, I concentrated on one thing and one thing only: passing my Series 6 and 63.

You have to wait thirty days before you can retake the test, and I planned to be back at the testing center on day thirty-one. When my testing date finally arrived, I felt ready, but I had learned the hard way that there were no guarantees. That morning, I woke up to one of the biggest snowstorms the city of Columbus had ever seen. With twenty-three inches of snow on the ground, half of the city had shut down. It wouldn't have been unreasonable for me to reschedule my test, but I'd spent most of my life living in areas where that kind of snow wasn't unusual. Besides, I had already jumped off a cliff and landed in the ocean, and I wanted to see if, when it came down to it, I would sink or swim.

At the testing center, I put my things in a locker, handed over my ID, and sat down at my computer terminal. Yes, I felt more prepared than I had the first time, but I also felt a lot more pressure. If I failed again, I'd only have one more shot. I had sacrificed a lot to get to this moment, and I wasn't taking any chances. I read each question carefully and triple-checked my answers. After more than three hours, I clicked on the button to finish and see my score.

As the computer whirred and processed my results, my heart beat faster. I held my breath and closed my eyes. Finally, I peeked at the screen.

I had passed.

"Yeah!" I yelled. "Hell yeah!" Then I remembered I was in the testing center and calmed myself down.

My life had just changed. All my dreams of owning my own business were coming true. And I had made it through an exhausting, demanding processes to make it happen. As I left the center, I couldn't contain my excitement. I yelled again, "Yeah!" and, laughing at the thrill of my achievement, I leapt into a snowbank.

Throughout February, March, and April of 2008, I lived out of a Dallas hotel. I was going through training, looking for a location for my office, interviewing, and putting everything I had into designing the systems and processes that would help me make my new agency a success. Tamika and I had sold the home we lived in. I would be moving to Texas, and she was off playing for the WNBA in Connecticut and looking to take advantage of a coaching opportunity in Kansas. We were the go-getter couple, both of us out making big things happen for our careers. I figured plenty of people made long-distance relationships work, and since we were married and committed to each other, everything would work out for us too. We were both taking our individual paths to conquer the world, but we were sure those paths would eventually lead us back together. We were so naive.

CHAPTER SIXTEEN

It's not the load that breaks you down; it's
the way you carry it. —Lou Holtz

My first year living in Dallas was a whirlwind. Many nights, I
interviewed applicants until eight o'clock and then worked on
the rest of my launch plan for the agency until well past midnight.
As I assembled my organization, I looked for people who would be
hungry, teachable, and willing to run through a wall for me once I
showed them I was ready to do the same for them. From the beginning,
I wanted the Raymond Agency to serve as an incubator that would
nurture the long-term career goals of each team member.

It took several weeks to lock in the people, but I was more than
satisfied with who I brought on board. My launch team consisted of
three full-time employees, one intern, and me. Two of those full-timers
were completely green. They had no experience in insurance at all, but
they had a couple of important things going for them. One, they were
English-Spanish bilingual, which allowed us to tap into Dallas's large
Spanish-speaking population, and two, they hadn't learned any bad

habits that I'd have to undo. My final full-timer came from another agency and had experience in the industry.

Together, the five of us spent a month and a half in the planning and training phase. Over those six weeks, I required everyone to come up with his or her own hot list. This list included influencers, prospective clients they could call on, individuals they could talk to about our products and services, and people and organizations we could potentially team up with in the community.

I hadn't forgotten my promise to myself. Once I landed my agency, I was taking it to number one, and going in to our first month, I set incredibly high goals. In my experience, most people underestimated what they could achieve in sports, in life, and in business. They failed to challenge themselves, so they failed to reach their maximum potential. On the other hand, winners raised the bar and didn't stop until they sailed over it. I was building a team of winners.

When I announced our goals for our first month, my new people had no reaction. Whatever number of quotes or applications I told them they needed to hit, they assumed it was reasonable. However, my experienced team member gave me a questioning look, and I knew I had to shut down her doubts right away. Talent can win the game, but ultimately teamwork wins championships. I needed everyone one hundred percent on board.

After our team meeting, I pulled her aside to explain to her how I worked and what I expected. "Listen. Whatever you do, you have to go full speed ahead," I told her. "I'm sure you're used to lower goals, but I don't want to hear anything negative about the goals I set for us. I need you to have a strong mindset, and I don't want to see it waver."

I assured her that, in return for her dedication, I would give her all the support she needed to reach new heights. Our other team members would look to her as an example. She was the one with the experience, and if she showed doubt, it could shake their confidence. Fortunately, she took the conversation well, and we got back to business.

When you set out to accomplish something big, you have to clear the mind of all negativity. If you have a positive mindset, work your tail off, and maintain the right attitude, great things will come. As long as my team members brought their best every day, they'd done their part. After that, it was up to their coach to lead them to the Promised Land. I was ready to train them, challenge them, motivate, and reward them to get us there. Nothing was going to stand in our way.

On August 1, 2008, the Raymond Agency officially opened its doors. We had already spent weeks preparing, and that first month, we gave it everything we had. In the end, we won. Each of us hit or exceeded our goals. In reaching for the unreachable, we also broke the company record for the most applications sold in an agency's first month. It was a huge win for me, but it may have been even more meaningful for my team. It proved to them that they were capable of more than they'd ever thought possible and that they'd been right to trust my leadership. All of the advance planning, intense training, role playing, setting up systems, and executing day after day had paid off.

It was really important to me that everyone on my team understood how much I appreciated their faith in me and the hard work they'd put in to make the Raymond Agency a success. To celebrate our record-breaking month, I took them all out on the town. A limo picked us up and drove us to the W Hotel, where we celebrated with cocktails in the lounge and enjoyed a luxurious dinner. That month set the tone for how we would operate as a business, and that dinner set the tone for what kind of boss I would be. We were off to a great beginning.

To continue to hit the numbers I had in mind, I needed to quickly build my network in Dallas. That meant that when I wasn't working, I was on the run all the time. I attended meetings of important organizations, like the Urban League and the local Chamber of Commerce, and connected with other business owners. I went out to the hottest restaurants and lounges, where Dallas VIPs hung out and connected. If the Cowboys or Mavericks were playing, I was probably in the stands. I attended black-tie charity events, where I met many of the city's most influential residents and found opportunities to serve in the community.

I wasn't out socializing for the fun of it. When Dallas decision-makers thought of insurance, I wanted them to think of me. When I walked in the room, I wanted people to say, "That's the insurance guy over there, Ben Raymond. You need to talk to him." I worked hard to create a brand for myself as the guy who insured all of Dallas's VIPs, business owners, professional athletes, and stars, and I did it without forgetting about the working and middle-class people who needed our products and services too.

As I was discovering, owning a business can easily consume your entire life, especially in launch phase, when you're trying to establish a solid foundation. It's easy to wake up early, drive to the office before rush hour starts, eat all your meals at your desk, run to meetings and events, go home and work until you fall out, and then wake up and do it all over again. Sometimes it's absolutely necessary to go hard like that, but a life that's all about work eventually becomes no life at all.

My marriage was in a sort of holding pattern during this time. The two of us lived in different states and spent more time apart than together. We both had careers that easily took up all of our time. However, family was still a priority in my life. My mother and Derrel continued to do well in Columbus, and as I built my business, I was also building my relationships with Slim and Davida.

My father had just over a year left before he'd be released from prison, and as we discussed his options, Dallas seemed more and more like the best place for him to get a fresh start. A visit from my sister would solidify the idea for us all.

———

Davida traveled to Dallas to celebrate New Year's Eve of 2009 with me. After a year of running non-stop, I was really looking forward to showing my sister and the guy she was dating a good time. We all went out together, but I took an immediate disliking to her boyfriend. I didn't know a lot about him, but I knew his type. I'd seen my mother date enough of the wrong men to know he was one of them.

Still, my sister was a grown woman, and she could date who she wanted. We all had a good time ringing in the New Year, and they went back to their hotel to get some rest. I spent the night at another hotel nearby, but before long my phone rang. A woman's anxious voice was on the other end. At first, I didn't realize who she was because she was talking so fast. Finally, I recognized the voice. It was a friend of Davida's who had gone out with us.

"You're not going to believe this, Ben," she said. "He hit her! Davida's crying and screaming. She's really hurt, but she doesn't want to call you. She's scared you'll do something crazy!"

I didn't waste time asking questions. I hung up the phone and tore down to my sister's hotel.

From the moment I met that guy, I'd had a bad feeling about him, but I had also underestimated his stupidity. That he would think he could put his hands on my sister while they were staying right down the road from me meant he'd underestimated me too. He clearly had no idea how much I loved Davida or how much I hated a man who thought he had the right to beat, choke, or bully a woman into submission.

It had been a long time since I had that much rage coursing through me, but I felt that old familiar feeling I'd gotten when Jimmy Shepherd would send my mother home with black eyes and bruises. I wanted to kill Jimmy back then, but I had been too young to be any threat to him. That day, as I raced to my sister's hotel, I wanted to kill her boyfriend too. The difference was that I wasn't a little boy anymore. I could tear him apart.

Luckily for all of us, the boyfriend was gone when I got to the hotel. Things could have gotten really ugly if I'd found him. I would have stomped him through the floor with no regrets. My sister was a tougher woman than my mother had ever been, but she was still a woman, and when I knocked on her door, I found a shaken, beaten-down version of her. Scars and bruises marked her neck and face. She looked like a scared, broken little girl.

Police officers came to the hotel to take my sister's complaint and photograph her wounds for evidence. When they were done, I drove Davida to my home and took her phone from her. Experience told me the so-called boyfriend would be blowing her up, trying to figure out where she was and begging her to come back to him. If the begging didn't work, he'd switch to threats and then back to apologies.

As she and I talked, Davida explained that he was an on-again, off-again drug dealer and he was on probation. It sickened me that my sister thought a loser like that was all she deserved.

He must have called more than sixty times over the course of a few hours. When I finally answered, I didn't plan to have a long conversation with him. I only had one question. "Did you put your hands on my sister or not?"

He sounded like he had a lot of practice trying to talk himself out of trouble because he immediately launched into a story filled with excuses that made him sound like the victim. "You know how your sister is. She put her hands on me first, and—"

"Yes or no?" I asked.

"Look," he said. "You guys got this beautiful relationship with your dad because you gave him a second chance. Me and Davida were arguing, and you know, she just kept pushing. But Davida knows I care about her. I just want her to give me a second chance too."

"If you ever put hands on my sister again," I told him, "I will kill you!"

I was angry, but I wasn't out of control. I knew exactly what I was saying. Of course, I wasn't going to kill the man. I wanted to leave no doubt in his mind that my sister had a man in her life who cared about her and was willing to go to war for her.

I also wanted Davida to hear exactly what I said so she would know that, even though she and I hadn't grown up together, we were still family. I had her back in all things, and I would do anything I had to do to protect her. I had my say, hung up the phone, and turned it off so I could talk to Davida without any more interruptions.

There was one thing I knew for sure and had to get out of the way. I could say whatever I wanted to him. I could call the police or his probation officer. I could keep my sister's phone from her or block his number. None of that would matter if she still wanted to be with him. If Davida chose to go back to this sorry-ass, woman-beating, drug dealer, I couldn't stop her.

I sat in a chair directly from where Davida reclined on the couch, and I looked her in the eyes. "Davida, do you want this to stop?" I asked. "If the answer is yes, I've got a solution for you. But if you want to be with him, or you tell me you don't know what you want, there's nothing I can do to help you."

Even though I'd lived with it as a child, I had never understood the psychology of a woman-beater. The weakness of a man who had to strike, slap, choke, hit, or shove a woman to try to control her made no sense to me. Not only was the man almost always physically stronger than the woman, a grown man should have a strength of mind and character that would make it unthinkable for him to hit a woman. If she was out of control, he could always remove himself from the situation rather than escalating it. If he had to, he could subdue her without hurting her. Yes, my sister could be aggressive, but a grown man should know how to handle that without resorting to violence.

"Do you want out of this?" I asked my sister again.

Davida nodded her head. She assured me that, yes, she was done being abused.

As I'd promised her, I had a plan. I called her boyfriend's probation officer and had him picked up for violating his probation. In the meantime, my sister moved in with me. I was still living alone, with Tamika coming down for weekend visits when she could, so it wasn't an imposition. I was happy to have Davida with me, and rather than let her risk going back to her home, where she might cross paths with her abuser, we sent for Aniah and enrolled her in school in Dallas.

It was a new beginning for both of Davida and Aniah, and in the years that followed, I would be increasingly proud of the way my sister made the most of the change. She would forge her path in a new city, perhaps surprising even herself with what she could accomplish. She had broken away from a bad situation, and for her, there was no looking back.

CHAPTER SEVENTEEN

People don't care what you know
until they know you care.

Early in 2009, my sister and my niece officially moved to Dallas, and so did Tamika. She retired from playing ball, and after living apart for most of the first two years of our marriage, we were finally residing in the same home as husband and wife. She needed some time to figure out what her next career move would be, and I wanted to give her that space and support her in whatever she decided to pursue.

When Tamika moved in with me, we essentially had to reintroduce ourselves to each other. Though we were legally a married couple, our respective lives had taken decidedly single tracks. We had both grown a lot over that time apart, but not as a couple. Individually, we were experiencing a long list of major life changes within a very short period of time. Tamika relocated to a new city. I was deeply invested in building a new business. Tamika wrestled with the options for her next career. I still had an intense journey of relationship building underway with my father, my sister, and the rest of our family on his side. Slim would be getting out of prison, and I was helping him plan where he would go and what he would do.

I was caught up in my world. Tamika was caught up in hers. At that time, I didn't recognize that she and I had become like two ships passing on a dark sea, unaware that we were both headed for the rocks. I may have noticed a few signs here and there, but I dismissed them as no big deal or chalked them up to the two of us needing more time to adjust.

Even though my marriage wasn't exactly flourishing, I was incredibly blessed in other areas of my life, including my growing business, my relationships with my father, sister, and niece, and my financial well-being, and I wanted to pay all of that forward. The longer I lived in Dallas the more opportunities I discovered to give back in ways big and small.

In the summer of 2009, my company was a sponsor for the Steve and Marjorie Harvey Foundation's camp for adolescent boys who were being raised by single mothers. As the sponsor representative, I went out and spoke to the campers. At the time, I had no idea how that one decision would affect me. I would come back to the camp year after year, and in the end, it would be a place where I would create some of my best memories, learn new things about my own identity, and meet people who would change the course of my life.

In the meantime, I also partnered with a local high school to create an internship program. I started out with twelve students, and frankly, it was absolute chaos. I felt like wild horse wrangler than a coach. Initially, it took a lot of effort to rein them all in and corral their focus. It was a bumpy beginning, but I redefined the internship program as we went along, and I figured out how to make it work for everyone involved.

Around the same time, I also started mentoring several young men, as I'd done in other cities, and I found myself offering them guidance about everything from how to ask a girl out to how to not end up as a teenage father. We talked about how to apply for a job and why it was important to maintain a fresh haircut and dress like you had some self-respect. I brought many of them into my office so they could see how a business was run and how a team worked together. As they approached the college application process, I had college students come in and help them not only apply to college but also apply for as many scholarships as possible. There was always another life skill or phase they needed to learn about, and I shared what knowledge I had or provided access to resources they needed.

Many of these boys were growing up just like I had. They had mothers who were doing their best for them, but their fathers were either absent or only half-engaged. More than anything else, I tried to provide much of what I'd missed, a man to talk to openly and honestly and some guidance when they needed it. I knew this mentoring work was a calling for me, and it became a way of life.

As much the young mentees benefited, working with them also caused me to stretch myself in new ways. I became a big brother, a fun uncle, and a giver of tough love all rolled into one. I celebrated my mentees achievements and helped them get back up after a disappointment, and along the way, I watched them grow into men.

———

As I became more established in Dallas, I also discovered new ways to have a positive impact. Basketball without Borders, a nonprofit organization with community outreach programs on five continents, offered me a life-changing opportunity to travel to Malawi. The small nation, located in southeastern Africa, is bordered by Tanzania, Mozambique, and Zambia, and at the time we traveled there, it ranked as the third poorest nation in the world. It's a country filled with beautiful landscapes, culture, and people and plagued by heart-rending deprivation.

My time in Malawi completely changed my view of the poverty I'd seen in America and other nations with highly developed economies. Of course, we had homeless and hungry people right in our own backyards, but what I witnessed in Malawi was different. I walked past kids lying on the side of the road, unmoving and unattended. I learned that a third of the country's children would never even start primary school.

Because of the food shortage and a lack of medical care in Malawi, the average life expectancy was only sixty-three years, compared to seventy-nine years in the United States. Over a million children, in a nation of only fifteen million people, were orphans. Most of those children had lost their parents to the HIV/AIDS epidemic, and one out of ten adults lived with the disease.

By American standards, buying my clothes in thrift stores, living in government-subsidized housing, and receiving public assistance had defined me as poor when I was a kid. I had sometimes seen myself that way too, but within a few hours of arriving in Malawi, I felt a profound appreciation for every cold deli sandwich I'd had for dinner and every second-hand pair of jeans I'd worn as a child. My mother and I had always had the safety nets of government aid, her family, and our community to ensure we had a roof over our heads and never felt the gnawing ache of true hunger.

Our mission in Malawi was two-fold. First, we wanted to promote leadership, friendship, character development, and the thrill of competitive sports in the Malawian communities. Local boys and girls were invited to participate in basketball camps and life-skills workshops. Second, we provided insecticide-treated bed nets (ITNs) to help reduce the incidence of malaria in the country and especially among young children, who were more likely to die from contracting the disease.

During the trip, we met a white American woman who worked for the State Department and had been in the country for several months. She had a passion for her work, but she held herself out as the expert on all things African in the way that can make privileged Americans seem entitled and condescending. After living in Malawi for a short while, she claimed she identified as an African and felt perfectly at home.

It didn't take long for some of us traveling with the organization to get tired of hearing just how Malawian she was. Finally, we decided to challenge her to prove how much she had assimilated. We dared her to eat the most common street food we'd seen during our stay.

"You really feel like one of the people?" my friend asked her. "Why don't you eat one of those sundried mice?"

In fact, I promised to pay her one hundred fifty dollars if she could do it.

"No problem," she said. "I'll do it."

Sundried mice were sold on sticks, like shish kebab. I'd treated one of my drivers to five of them, for which he'd been quite grateful, but the idea of sinking my teeth into one made my stomach flop.

"You sure?" my friend asked.

The woman bobbed her head up and down. She was determined to prove her point—and win the money.

I just shook my head. I couldn't imagine it was going to turn out well.

We all watched as she bit through hair and skin and into the flesh of the dead mouse. She may have gotten through two bites before it hit her. I don't know how much mouse she swallowed, but she spent the rest of the day throwing up.

I wish I could say I felt sorry for her, but that would be a lie. My friend and I may have even shared a laugh or two at her expense. Playing with cultural appropriation in the way that she had was offensive, demeaning, and annoying. Hopefully, it was a lesson learned the hard way for her.

Aside from that stereotypical "arrogant American" moment, the trip could only be described as a success. Meeting the people of Malawi and understanding how that nation was representative of many others with similar needs opened my mind to a bigger vision of the ways in which I could be a force for good in the world. It also made me appreciate the life I had more than ever before.

———

Two years after I moved to Dallas, I wasn't the same man I'd been when I got there. I'd seen so much more of the world, discovered what it was really like to have the freedom and responsibility of running my own business, and grown in my roles as brother and uncle. In 2010, I would finally get the opportunity to fully experience and enjoy my role as my father's son.

On a sunny May day, Davida and I parked at the train station in the heart of downtown Dallas, and got out to meet our father as he took a few more steps toward his freedom. We took turns recording the moment on video, documenting the first time the three of us had ever been together outside of prison walls.

Dressed in baggy jeans, a hat, and a polo shirt, Slim carried a camouflage duffel bag slung over his shoulder. The bag was filled with everything he'd accumulated during his sentence, small items that he'd bought with the money from his job in the prison kitchen, things that meant a lot to him inside, but the value of which would fade as he found the whole world opening up to him again.

We had decided to let Slim take the train from Pekin to Dallas because it would buy him a lot more time on his own than the short flight would have. I figured he'd enjoy watching the open land go by outside his window and have some time to think about the adjustment he'd be making in the coming days. The outside world had changed dramatically since he'd last been a part of it.

When my father entered federal prison, all cell phones were flip phones, email and chat rooms were the most common ways to communicate with people online, and less than half of Americans had regular Internet access. It was the same year the hanging chad was blamed for Al Gore losing the presidential election to George W. Bush.

By the time Slim was released in 2010, Americans were surfing the Internet with their smart phones and connecting with long-lost classmates and exes on a site called Facebook. Almost seventy-five percent of us had Internet access, and the video calls that science-fiction writers had once dreamed about were commonplace. The country also had its first black president.

So much had changed while my father served his sentence. Even though inmates were exposed to all of these innovations through the media, experiencing this new world firsthand would be different. While time may have passed slowly for him inside, the outside world had sped up. It would take some time for him to adjust.

While my father had missed out on my journey to manhood, I was doing all I could to ensure that our relationship continued to grow. He would have to spend six months living in a halfway house, but we were able to get an exception to allow him to reside in a Dallas halfway house for that period of time. For the first time, he, Davida, and I actually lived in the same city.

I wanted to make the most of my time with my father. In his early Dallas days and weeks, we went out to restaurants, where I treated him to the first decent meal he'd had in a decade. I took him shopping and brought him around to my office to meet the team.

I even took him to a strip club. After all, he'd been surrounded by nothing but men for ten years.

Once he completed his six months in the halfway house, Slim moved in with Tamika and me so we could help him get on his feet. As a convicted felon whose last decade of work experience had happened behind bars, he struggled to find employment. However, I was determined to make sure Slim had every opportunity to stay on the right track and avoid any situation that might cause him to slip back into his old ways.

Finally, I helped him land a job working at a plant, and Slim found his own apartment. He started going to church, and he spent most of his free time with us, his family. For all his ups and downs, my father was good company, and we had a lot of fun together. We went to Cowboys games and out to cocktails and dinner. We barbecued and spent a lot of time talking. Little by little, my father filled in the gaps in my knowledge of our family history.

There was something very surreal about those days in Dallas with Slim. There I was hanging out with the man I'd dreamed of meeting for so many years. Still, I knew my father had spent most of his adult life in and out of trouble with the law, and I wasn't totally convinced that he was done with that lifestyle. I guarded a piece of my heart in case he should backslide again, but I prayed that would never happen.

———

Just as I did what I could to help my father get to the place where he lived independently, I also wanted to help many of my team members get to the place where they no longer needed me. It may sound counterintuitive, but I knew most of the people who worked with me were only there for a season. Some would use their experience in the Raymond Agency to land new jobs or start a business. A few would go on to open their own agency.

In 2010, I coached two people through the rigorous process to secure their own agency opportunities, one in Houston, Texas, and another in Atlanta, Georgia. It was an extremely satisfying feeling to watch them go off and become business owners. Ultimately, their success was also my success no matter where it took them.

As we rolled into 2011, my agency was still going strong. My team and I continued to hit goals most people deemed unattainable, and we reaped the rewards of our hard work. Early in the year, I received the honor of making the top fifty in sales for my company, but the best of that year was still to come.

In November, I was selected by my peers for an honor that meant more to me than any recognition I'd received up to that point in my professional career. Based on my agency's performance and my community service, the company's agents voted for me to do represent us all and do the coin toss at the Bayou Classic. The annual game, which took place in New Orleans, was one of the biggest rivalries in the world of historically black colleges and universities. Because of its history and its significance, many fans referred to it unofficially as the "Black Super Bowl." Throughout Thanksgiving weekend, fashion shows, golf tournaments, pep rallies, parties, and parades led up to the big game. It was a big deal.

Being selected for the coin toss would have been a huge deal for anyone, but as a former athlete it had a special meaning for me. As I walked out on the field in the Superdome, the cheers of the crowd took me back to third grade, when I was scoring goals in soccer, back to ninth grade when I was making touchdowns, back to high school when local newspapers followed my basketball exploits and celebrated my achievements, and back to college when I played my way to team captain.

This time though, I wasn't being acknowledged for my athletic accomplishments. I was being recognized as Ben the man who put all of his knowledge and experience into building a successful business. The applause was for Ben the entrepreneur who went after his own dreams and helped his team achieve theirs. The cheers from my peers were for Ben the giver who had a heart for his community and would do all he could to help other young men and boys find their own path to success as only they could define it. This recognition was for me as a whole person. And it felt incredible.

CHAPTER EIGHTEEN

Your story is the greatest gift you can give.

I woke up just in time to watch the sun rise through the windshield of my SUV. Cursing under my breath, I sat up and tried to rub the kink out of my neck. I don't care how roomy an Escalade is to ride in; it was certainly no place for a grown man to sleep. Yet, there I was, Dallas's insurer to the stars, crunched up in the back seat of a car, in the parking lot of a very nice hotel. "What the hell am I doing?" I mumbled to myself as I climbed out and stretched my legs. The warmth of the morning sun didn't do much to improve my mood. I needed a toothbrush, a shower, and a massage.

The previous night, Tamika and I had clashed again, arguing about everything and nothing all at the same time, and it had gotten ugly. Frustrated with the bickering and our inability to end our marriage amicably, I threw my hands up, stormed out the door, hopped in my car, and sped off. When I rolled into the hotel parking lot, I was still pissed off. I sat there, staring at the entrance to the lobby. "Why should

I have to pay three hundred dollars for a hotel room?" I muttered. "I have enough bills already. I'm not doing it. To hell with that!"

In a moment of bullheadedness, I climbed into the back seat of my Escalade and slept there. It was the worst night of sleep I'd had in years. I flipped and flopped for hours, shifting around as I tried to fit my long legs and arms into some kind of comfortable position. The whole thing reminded me too much of the times in my childhood when I didn't know where I'd spend the night. I had come too far to live with that kind of chaos and uncertainty.

In reality, our marriage had ended almost a year before that night, in early 2012. In 2011, I'd soared to incedible highs in my business, but as the year ended, I'd entered a major low in my personal life. Five years after I'd said "I do," I found myself thinking more and more, "I don't." I could have blamed our failing marriage on our youthful naiveté, career pressures and the distractions of our individual ambitions, the many months we'd spent living apart, or all of the above. All of the life changes Tamika and I had undergone had created a gulf between us that we couldn't figure out how to bridge. A husband and wife should make each other better people. Somehow, we found ourselves doing just the opposite.

Since childhood, I'd been accustomed to dealing with problems on my own and protecting my privacy, and as my marriage ended, I withdrew from the world. I still had a business to run, but I spent a lot of time alone. I needed time to process my own sense of failure. I had never imagined my marriage would end in divorce, but there was no saving it. I had to do some self-assessment and figure out what part I'd played in our unhappy ending. I needed to work on myself so I could learn from this loss and come out of it a better man.

As the calendar flipped over to 2012, I began a season of personal transformation. The pending divorce had opened my eyes to a need to shift my priorities. I felt called to play at a higher level in every area of my life, and I was committed to change. I started with the things I could most easily control, and at the top of my list was my health. I got serious about eating right for the first time, and I dropped thirty pounds of fat within a few months. My physical health was just one part of the equation though. I also developed a new, clearer vision for my future.

That stage of my life was emotionally and mentally draining, and my retreat into self-reflection allowed me to recuperate and take care of myself. Because of our financial obligations, assets we'd accumulated during the marriage, and family ties, we remained in the same home while we negotiated our way out of the relationship. Living under the same roof while building separate lives only increased the strain, but the decision had been made. It was only a matter of time and working our way through the legal processes. In the meantime, I kept myself busy with work and stayed away from home as much as possible.

I didn't see my family as much during that time, but I needed space to heal and grow, and I connected with them when I could. One afternoon, I got a call from Mom Kat that really shook me. She wanted to tell me that she and Hugh were also going through a divorce. It turned out that they were further along in the process than I was. The news hit me hard not because I'd thought their marriage was perfect—no marriage is—but because both Mom Kat and Hugh had played pivotal roles in my life.

I loved all of the Hughes family, every one of them, but my bond with Mom Kat ran deeper than anything. The end of their marriage saddened me, but my first priority was Mom Kat's well-being. When Hugh and I spoke later, I asked him, man to man, regardless of what had happened between the two of them, to please look out for her and treat her fairly. I could only imagine how difficult it was for the two of them to call it quits after more than two decades of living as husband and wife. I still hadn't told Mom Kat that my own marriage was over, and it would be some time before I opened up about it.

Several months later, while I was in Milwaukee on business, I drove down to Oshkosh. An important part of my plan for personal transformation was to better understand the journey I'd gone through as a child. Back in the small city where I was born and raised, I visited the apartments and duplexes my mother and I had lived in over those turbulent years. Of course, I remembered the difficult times—the loneliness, sadness, and fear—but I also recalled those years when my mother was at her very best.

So often, what came easily to most people required tremendous effort from her, but she never gave up. Her determination to be a mother for me kept her fighting to find her way back to her healthiest self. I realized how easy it would have been for her to give up and lose me to foster care for good. From a young age, she'd been dealt a tough hand. My mother had suffered, and in her pain, she'd made some mistakes. But even when she struggled to love herself, she had always loved me.

I went back to Grace Lutheran, where I saw the records I set playing for the Wildcats still on display in the trophy case. While I was there, I ran into the kindergarten teacher I'd had such a huge crush on as a kid, and I couldn't help smiling when she remembered me right away. "You guys were my favorite class," she told me. Everywhere I went, I took pictures, and it was a fun moment to take a picture with the teacher I'd fallen head over heels for as a six-year-old boy.

During that trip, I also joined Mom Kat, Hugh, Evan, and Tommy at the White House for one last, nostalgic family meal. The entire family sat around the dining table, enjoying another lavish Hughes dinner, reliving memories, laughing, and having a good time. We went out in Oshkosh that night and ran into Chad, who joined our festivities. He had gone through some rough times since we graduated high school together, but that guy everyone thought was trouble had begun to turn his life around. Chad still liked to party, but he had gotten involved in real estate, acquiring rental properties, and he was on the verge of building something great.

It was a special night—a lot like the old days, but with so many things changed in our lives—and a perfect way to say goodbye to an end of an era. The Hugheses were selling the home where I'd felt so welcomed and loved, the place where I'd finally found a family. Mom Kat had decided to move to Milwaukee to live near Evan. Tommy was going on with his life in New Orleans, and Hugh was entering his next chapter as a newly single man. I hated that the Hughes family was being reconfigured in such a sad way, but I was still so grateful to forever be a part of it.

———

One of the ways I stayed positive during that rocky time was by continuing my community service work. Speaking and mentoring were ways I fulfilled my purpose, and turning my focus outward reminded me of how blessed I still was. As summer of 2012 rolled around, I volunteered for my third year with the Steve Harvey Mentoring Program for Young Men, a national camp for teenage boys being raised by single moms. It had been a positive experience for me so far, but I realized I needed to contribute more.

After my first experience at the camp, in 2009, I'd felt like it was a special place with a unique mission, a place where I could have a positive influence on lots of young lives. It inspired me to launch my own charitable foundation, and it sparked a desire in me to do more for the campers. That first year, I gave Mr. Harvey a quick, bullet-point version of my story. I felt compelled to give Mr. Harvey a glimpse of my journey from foster care to business ownership so he could understand who I really was. "I'm here as a sponsor," I'd told him, "but I relate to these boys on a deeper level. I know they can learn something from my journey."

For the first time in my life, in the summer of 2010, I had stood in front of a group of people and told the truth of my life story without shame or embarrassment. The previous year, I'd come to the camp to warn the campers about the dangers of texting and driving. It was an important lesson, one that could save lives, and I hoped it had really hit home with them each time. But this was different.

This was me, standing before a group of young men as a college-educated business owner who truly understood where they were coming from and what they were going through. I had been on public assistance. I had dealt with my mother's drug addiction, her mental illness, and her violent, criminal boyfriends. I had spent my childhood feeling like something was wrong with me because my father had abandoned me. I had been bullied and shoved aside for being different. I understood the heartache, the anger, and the self-doubt many of the young boys had experienced in their own lives.

The reactions from the campers when I shared the raw truth of my childhood convinced me that my story could make a difference to the people who needed to hear it most. In the coming months and years, I would share it again and again, often in professional settings, where I saw looks of recognition in the eyes of grown men and women who saw their own history in parts of mine. After one event, an executive came up to me and thanked me for my honesty. He explained that his father was dead and buried but the executive was still so wounded by their relationship that he couldn't bring himself to stop by the cemetery and visit his father's grave. I completely understood his mixed feelings. "If you don't want to do it alone," I told him, "I can go with you."

My decision to open up to a group of kids who needed guidance made as much of a difference for me as it did for them. It changed the way I connected with people, and it helped me to continue to heal. I had gone back in 2011, and I was happy to do it again for the 2012 camp session.

———

On a sunny Saturday afternoon, I once again addressed an audience of nearly one hundred young males on the brink of manhood. The next day, I came back for the camp's closing ceremony, and I was talking with a football player, when a young woman walked by. She spoke to us, but when she heard him making some obnoxious comments about women, she removed herself from the conversation.

That woman was Karli Harvey, Steve Harvey's daughter, and while she did a lot of work for the foundation and for the camp, it was our first time meeting. Somehow, we'd missed each other completely over the previous three summers. It was June 16, 2012, and though neither of us had a clue what the future held, I had just encountered the woman I would spend the rest of my life with. Later, Karli would admit to me that she watched me drive away that day as we were both leaving. I teased her that she must have been waiting to see if I left in a nice car before she decided if she was interested in me or not. But in truth, on that day, I was just another speaker, and she was another member of camp leadership.

After the camp's closing ceremony the next day, Karli and I exchanged contact information in hopes that our foundations could partner in some way. Over the following weeks, we talked a little about what we had going on. In one phone conversation she told me, "You know, you're long winded. Why don't you just send me a follow-up email?" I laughed at her honesty because, even though she was sort of right, it was bold of her to say it. I always liked a straight shooter.

Over the summer months, our paths continued to cross. Karli and I were both in New Orleans for Essence Festival, an annual music and empowerment event, which took place around July 4th. Karli put on a fashion show as one of the festival events, and my friends and I stopped by to check it out and lend a little support. I was impressed by what I saw, but clearly in her element, Karli was busy working. I didn't want to interrupt her, so I slipped out. Later, she told me that she had spotted me there in the back corner with my friends.

We chatted, texted, and emailed periodically, but we didn't talk a lot or actually get together until I took a trip to Atlanta, where she lived, to visit a friend. I invited Karli to dinner at STK, a steakhouse and lounge, and she agreed to join me. It was so nice to spend time with someone who said exactly what she thought and made it easy for me to do the same. We shared a love of fashion, and I was enjoying her company, so I also invited her to go to mall with me so we could hang out while I shopped. That weekend, I really took notice of how warm her energy was. I felt my own mood elevate just from being with her.

Later that summer, when the Neighborhood Awards, a star-studded, four-day extravaganza, took place in Las Vegas, some of my friends wanted to hit the performances and parties. I thought I'd give it a shot and see if Karli could get me tickets to some of the events, since the whole thing was produced under her father's brand. I sent her a text asking for the favor, and her response came back:

"I'll see what I can do." I chuckled to myself and waited to see if she would come through.

My company was a sponsor for the event, so I attended the live on-air broadcast of the *Steve Harvey Morning Show*, and Karli did get me tickets for another event as well as an after-party. When we finally met up, everyone was dressed to go out, but Karli was wearing a "STAFF" shirt. She had warned me that everyone working the event had to wear them, but I thought she meant the frontline people. I had to give her a hard time about it because she really looked ridiculous.

"You're representing a sponsor," she said. "Please do me a favor and call and complain about how dumb I look."

Later, we found a quiet bar, where we once again fell into easy, open conversation. We talked about important things, like our life goals and relationship experiences, and frivolous things too. She was as much fun and she had been whenever we connected, but something was different. I had always seen Karli as a beautiful, stylish, intelligent woman, but that night, there was something more between us. That night, there was chemistry.

———

By the time my birthday rolled around in October, Karli and I were officially a couple. That Christmas, she invited me home to spend the holiday with her and some of her family, including her father, stepmother, and siblings. She told them all she'd invited a guest to dinner, but she didn't tell her father who that guest was. "It's someone I've been seeing for a while," she'd hinted, "someone you know from the camp."

When I pulled up to the house on Christmas Day, I was meeting Mr. Harvey for the first time as his daughter's love interest. I rang the doorbell and waited, expecting Karli to answer and usher me in. But that didn't happen.

When the door opened, Mr. Harvey was standing there, and when he saw me, he shut the door in my face. Luckily, he opened it again, and he was laughing good-naturedly as he let me in. After dinner, I found him in his office and stepped inside to talk. As I expected, he wanted to know what my intentions were for his daughter.

I was as transparent and upfront with Mr. Harvey as I had been with Karli. I explained to him that, yes, I'd had a difficult upbringing. I'd seen my mother and my sister abused, and I hated that kind of violence and manipulation. It went against everything I believed was right. I told him more about my business and my plans for the future. And I also let him know that I was not yet officially divorced. "We're still in the same house, but it's been over for a more than a year. We're just figuring out the finances," I explained. "I want to be as fair as possible, but I also have to be careful not to destroy what I've built so far."

"I know how those things go," he told me. "There's no perfect scenario."

I felt fortunate that Mr. Harvey had gotten to know me as a speaker, a businessman, and a mentor before I started to date his daughter. He knew how hard I'd worked for everything I had. He'd had a chance to see my integrity, professionalism, and sincere heart for service before I came knocking on his door, and I'm sure it made it easier for him to give me the tentative thumbs-up to pursue my relationship with Karli.

Karli had a whole family I needed to win over, but the top two gatekeepers were certainly her dad and her twin sister, Brandi. Karli and Brandi were incredibly close and had even gone to college together. Luckily, Brandi was supportive of our relationship from the beginning.

More than anything, she wanted to see her sister loved, cared for, and happy, and I promised to do everything in my power to be the man who made Karli feel all of those things.

We were off to a great beginning, but Karli and I had one big challenge to overcome. We had to find a way to bridge the distance between Atlanta, where she lived, and Dallas, where I lived. Because I had seen firsthand how easy it was for a long-distance relationship to fall apart, I asked Karli to commit with me to seeing each other at least once every three weeks and staying in touch in between. That connection was a non-negotiable for me, and she agreed that if we were going to see where the relationship led us, we had to take it seriously. We had to give it the time and attention it needed to grow and flourish.

I appreciated that Karli had the maturity to understand that our relationship needed that real investment from both of us. I also loved that she was all in on the personal transformation journey I'd begun. She lent her support and advice to help me progress faster in areas where she was strongest, and she was open to receiving the same kind of motivation and guidance from me. With that kind of partnership, I was excited to see what our future held.

———

While Karli and I were establishing our relationship, the divorce negotiations dragged on. Not long after that night in the Escalade I moved into my own condo, and one of the first things I bought was the most highly rated luxury mattress I could find. Every time I lay across it, that mattress served as a reminder that I could never go backwards in my life. I'd attained a level of success and a standard of living that I was willing to fight to maintain, and that included sleeping well, in a comfortable bed, under my own roof.

Going through the divorce had also revealed to me the true colors of some of the people I had called friends. It would have been unfair and immature of me to ask anyone to choose sides, but some of the support and concern I'd expected was non-existent from almost as soon as people learned what was happening. People who used to call me all the time disappeared almost overnight, and I realized what I had thought was loyalty was something else entirely. Friendship that only lasts in the good times is worthless. My friendship with Al, on the other hand, had grown since he first introduced me to the insurance business, and he was one of the few people I could confide in and turn to. He cautioned me to be careful who I trusted.

One night, alone in my condo, I sat on the edge of my bed and thought about who really belonged in my circle. So many people had surprised me by the way they turned their backs or even tried to tear me down or damage my business, but I took it all as a lesson learned. I was ready to clean house, but I decided to put it in God's hand. I dropped to my knees and prayed, "Lord, you know my heart, and you know everyone else's too. I don't want any fake people in my life anymore, Lord. Rid me of those people who shouldn't be there, and leave me surrounded by real friends who understand loyalty." I found peace in letting go.

It was all a part of the process. When a marriage ends, the breakup doesn't just affect the husband and wife. Although we didn't have any children, our parents and siblings, friends and relatives had believed in our relationship. We were each connected to people we'd come to love and care about through the marriage, and breaking the news to them hurt everyone involved. The biggest challenge for me was telling my niece, Aniah.

Everyone in the family worried about how Aniah would handle the news. They wanted to protect her from the truth for as long as possible, and out of respect for their wishes, I avoided telling her for several weeks. I understood their concerns about giving bad news to a young child, but what they failed to realize was that keeping the secret put me in a terrible position. I felt like I was losing my family. Aniah had become such an important part of my life, and I couldn't even have her over to my home for a visit or a sleepover. Whenever I saw her, I felt like I was lying to her, and I didn't like having any element of dishonesty in our relationship.

Finally, I let everyone know that we weren't doing Aniah any favors by letting her live with a lie. She had developed a close bond with Tamika, but my niece deserved to be told the truth. While she may not have known exactly what was going on, children aren't stupid. Whenever she visited the home Tamika and I had shared, Tamika would tell her that Uncle Ben was working or out of town. I'm sure Aniah picked up on something wrong in those stories, and she must have wondered what we were hiding from her.

One afternoon, I took Aniah and her cousin out to a restaurant and broke the news to her. "Uncle Ben has his own place now, but I understand if you don't want to visit yet," I told her. "If you need to, you can go home and think about it for a while. I just want you to know that you're always welcome at my place."

Across the table from me, my ten-year-old niece burst into tears. She had so few examples of happily married couples in her world. Davida had only been nineteen when she had her daughter, and the two of them had gone through a lot of instability. My marriage had provided a sense of the security Aniah craved. No one understood that need more than I did, and it broke my heart to have to disappoint my niece and snatch that security from her.

I did my best to reassure her. "We both still love you very much, and we'll both still be here for you, Aniah."

It was such a relief when she told me that she really wanted to see my new place that day. She was hurt, but she hadn't lost any of her love for me. We were still family.

————

Divorce is never good for anyone's bottom line, except for the accountants and attorneys involved. But I had prepared for the financial strain of untangling every asset and liability while splitting up our home. In 2012, my agency had been on track to reach company goals that would earn me a $30,000 bonus. That money would provide a little cushion to see me through the rest of the legal wrangling. I was counting on it.

Unfortunately, counting on something doesn't guarantee that it'll happen. Just a month before I expected to receive the bonus payout, my company liaison reached out to let me. She wanted to let me know that, in fact, I wouldn't see a penny of that money.

"What are you talking about?" I asked. "We clearly have the numbers."

She explained that, while I was right, we'd failed to meet the prerequisites. My agents didn't have the right licensing to make us eligible for the bonus. One of them had a license that was supposed to be transferred from another state, and that had never happened. The bonus could only be paid out to an agency with at least one properly licensed team member, not including the owner.

"I submitted that paperwork," I told her. "Everything was taken care of months ago."

It turned out that the paperwork had never been processed. I had assumed everything had gone fine, but I had been wrong. My liaison and I went back and forth on the issue, but at the end of the day, her message didn't change. *No license, no bonus.*

After she and I were done, I thought about what she'd said. My agency had performed incredibly well, but that didn't seem to matter to her. At no point in our conversation did she say, "Hey, Ben. I know you guys have worked hard for this. Let me see what I can do." I took her lack of support personally, and it infuriated me that she wouldn't back me up on something this important. But if she wasn't going to fight for me, I was damn sure going to fight for myself.

Someone in the system had dropped the ball, but I was prepared to recover their fumble. I went to work filing appeal after appeal based on the fact that we'd done everything right on our end. I came at it from every possible angle, but the final call went against me. *No license, no bonus.*

I'd made a decision at the outset of the divorce process that I wouldn't downgrade the lifestyle I'd worked so hard to achieve. Now, the money I'd been relying on to keep me whole had slipped right through my fingers. It hurt, but it was also a valuable lesson for me. As the business owner, I was always responsible for seeing that things were done right. The buck always stopped with me. From that point on, I had systems in place to keep that kind of thing from ever being overlooked again.

I'd lost that bonus, but I wasn't giving up on my commitment to myself. I went out and got a full-time sales job to supplement my income. At Stryker Medical, I sold medical equipment and furniture. Balancing the job and my agency meant I had to leave my house as early as 4:00 a.m. to drive to Oklahoma every day. Depending on where my account meetings took place, the commute lasted from one to three hours each way. I split my time to get maximum results from two full-time careers at once.

My team didn't know I was going through a divorce or that I had taken a second job. They watched me come in late every afternoon and thought, "Man, I can't wait to have my own thing and only work half-days." They had no idea how much I actually had on my plate. It was a lot to take on, but it was worth it to me. I only kept that job for about a year, but during my time with the company, I gave it everything I had. I was recognized as a top performer in my training group, and I went on to exceed the quotas for medical furniture sales. Working two full-time jobs wasn't fun, but I did what I had to do to keep moving forward.

———

One of the sticking points in the divorce had been a second agency I'd helped start in 2011. It was doing incredibly well, and in the end, I decided I had to bite the bullet and let it go. Regardless of how things had ended with us, I still wanted Tamika to win in life and I wanted to close the book on the divorce. In that spirit, I agreed that she could keep that agency. I made my peace with God, knowing that he had given me the ability to replace that business and build even more. As the divorce was finalized and my finances rebounded, I resigned my sales job and turned my energies back to growing my agency.

With more of my time freed up, I also invested in my relationship with Karli. Though we weren't ready to commit to marriage, I suggested that we go to relationship counseling together after we'd dated for a while. We'd both grown up in broken homes and seen our parents go through troubled relationships. I had learned in my first marriage that I still had issues of my own to resolve, and I wanted to go into the future with Karli as two healthy people who knew how to work together in good times and in bad.

Karli agreed that it was a good idea, and our time in counseling turned out to serve us incredibly well. We discovered a lot about each other and about ourselves during the process, and I was happy to learn that in the most important ways, we were very well matched.

Since moving to Dallas, I'd experienced some wonderful ups and some incredibly trying downs, but it felt like things had turned a corner. Slim was working and spending time with his family, including me. Davida was discovering how strong and capable she was, and Aniah was blossoming under so much love and attention. Back in Columbus, my mother and Derrell were doing better than I'd expected and as well as I'd hoped. All of that was capped off by finding new romance when I least expected it. Life was good, and I was grateful for all of it, but tragedy was lurking just beyond the horizon.

CHAPTER NINETEEN

Tough people stand taller in tough times.

The tap of dress shoes and heels clacking and shuffling across the tiled floor echoed through the halls as men and women in suits made their way to one proceeding or another. As I walked through the Dallas County courthouse, an unsettling mix of cautious hope, fear, and shock churned inside of me. Outside of this building, the rest of the world was consumed with shopping for last-minute gifts to finish up their Christmas list while they sang along with the carols playing over loudspeakers in every store. Fighting the crowds at the mall to pick out toys for Aniah, or standing in line at the post office to ship a box of presents to my mother and Derrel would have been a pleasure just then.

It was useless to try to predict what would happen inside the courtroom, but the thoughts came anyway. Would the judge show some compassion? Or would she bring down the hammer in a show of "tough on crime" justice? Would my day end with relief or tears?

A familiar voice snapped me out of my contemplation. "Ben? Hey, man! What are you doing here?"

I spun around to see my homeboy Justin, a prominent Dallas County prosecutor, right behind me. "You get yourself in a little trouble?" he asked, half joking and half concerned.

Justin had been a friend to me when I needed to understand the inner workings of the local criminal court system. I appreciated his support, but just then, I didn't have it in me to explain to him why I was there. "I can't really talk now," I told him. "I'll explain it to you later."

"No problem. Call me any time." Justin hurried on his way, calling out, "And Merry Christmas to you!"

I responded with a half-hearted, "Merry Christmas," in return.

Inside the courtroom, I took a seat on a long bench, almost like a church pew, in a gallery filled with people who were strangers to me. It wasn't long before the court was called to order and the judge took the bench. She was middle-aged black woman who was not known for showing mercy. In fact, she had a reputation as a "hanging judge," and rumor had it that, when her own son faced a criminal conviction, she'd sanctioned the harsh sentence handed down to him. My stomach twisted as fresh worries dampened that glimmer of hope I was trying to hold on to.

As case after case went up, and the judge handed out sentences, my anxiety grew. It hurt me to see all those families being torn apart, especially since so many of them were black families like mine, and I wondered if it affected the judge in any way at all. If she felt anything other than disdain, she didn't show it.

When my father's case was finally called, a bailiff escorted him in to sit next to his public defender. The evidence against my father included recordings of the phone calls between him and me while he was in jail. I had been so pissed at him for getting locked up again, and I let him know it on those calls.

"We set you up for success, and you threw it all away," I'd told him. "I got you a job, you couldn't show on time. I built that cleaning business around you, but you somewhere getting fucked up with that crackhead." As I listened to my voice played back to me, I couldn't help wondering if I had damaged my father's chances for freedom.

The prosecutor called me to the stand to question me about what I'd said. I swore to tell the truth, and I did. "I meant everything I said to my father. I was disappointed and angry with him," I explained, "but I also know he needs help. He's never had any kind of treatment for his addiction, and he needs a shot at rehabilitation." That was my plea for leniency. I wanted to say more, but what more could I say? And I couldn't read anything on this judge's face.

I couldn't tell if my testimony did my father any favors or not, but the proceeding moved quickly. The prosecutor had a tough, direct manner, and she went hard, painting Slim as an incorrigible drug dealer. She was so convincing that if I didn't know another side of my father, if I didn't love him, I might have believed they should throw the book at him. But it wasn't up to me. Two African-American women, the prosecutor and the judge, held my father's fate in their hands.

The morning had dragged by, but my father's sentencing progressed shockingly fast. This is a process that determines the fate of a man's life, altering his course forever. The sentence impacts his family just as much as it affects him. There was so much I wanted to say on our behalf, but I sat there, silent, nervous sweat beading on my neck as I listened, watched, waited, and yes, held on to hope. Finally, the judge looked down at my father and pronounced his punishment. When all was said and done, David "Slim" Brumfield, the father I'd finally found and reunited with after a lifetime of separation, was sentenced to twenty-five years in a Texas state prison.

———

I had seen my father's downfall coming for months, but I'd been powerless to stop it. Not long after his probation ended in early 2013, Slim's behavior began to change. The company he was keeping all of a sudden included a woman who was clearly on drugs. Out of nowhere, his cell phone became a hotline. He was getting calls at all hours of the day and night. More and more, I started to believe that my father was falling back into his drug addiction. The periodic drug testing that had forced him to stay clean while he was on probation had ended, and if he wanted to use, there was no one to stop him.

When Slim called me from jail to ask me to bail him out, I flat out refused, but I did visit him. After everything we'd done to help him get established, he was throwing it all away. I wanted to know what he had to say for himself.

"It's not like it seems. I didn't do it," Slim told me. "I was set up." He wanted me to go to his apartment to grab some important documents and whatever the woman he was seeing might sell to buy drugs. He also wanted me to find the two thousand dollars he had hidden in a jacket pocket in a closet in his apartment.

"You've got two thousand dollars, and you've been asking me for money?" I asked him, but given that we were talking in a jail, I shouldn't have been surprised by any secrets he'd kept.

I was furious with my father for messing up again, but I didn't want him to lose what little property and cash he'd accumulated since he got out of prison. I agreed to do him the favor, but at first, the apartment complex's manager refused to let me enter the apartment. I had to convince him I was a respectable business owner and wouldn't cause more problems. Inside, every room had been turned upside down. I stepped over piles of clothes and random household objects. The police don't clean up behind themselves after they search for evidence. The whole place was wrecked. And the money was gone.

With his cash missing, Slim had no money of his own, but his bond amount was fairly low, and my sister couldn't stand the idea of our father sitting in a jail cell again. She scraped up the money, which was a real sacrifice for her at the time, and bailed him out on her own. Slim moved in with Davida for a while, and although I felt like being done with him, I also felt like it was my responsibility to speak with him, man to man, about what he was doing to our family.

Getting arrested was not a wake-up call for my father. He treated my sister's place like a crash pad, staying out half the night, making her worry that he'd end up getting picked up by the police again. He'd tell her he was getting out of her way, but he'd run the streets for a few days and then pop back up at her place. When he came to me for rent money to get his own apartment, I helped him out more for her sake than his, but I also tried to get him to see how he was hurting Davida. I thought I could stay calm, but I was holding on to so much anger that the conversation quickly became a shouting match.

"You're using your family like you use those crackheads out on the street," I yelled at him. "What kind of man just uses women like that? Take this money, but if you mess up again, you know you're going to jail, right? And I don't want to hear nothing about how bad it is in there! I don't care if the food is shitty or you need money on your books. You make that choice to get locked up again, then it's on you!"

The two of us went back and forth for a while, but it was getting me nowhere. When I finally calmed down, I tried to get through to him, one last time, by appealing to his love for the girls. "Listen, Davida and Aniah, they look up to you," I told him. "They love you. Aniah's getting older, and she sees everything you do. What kind of example are you setting for her? You need to step up and be the man they need you to be. Stop hurting them."

My father finally gave a little "I'm ready for a change, son," he said. "I really am."

"Good," I said, "because if you go to jail, I'm not visiting you. I don't want to see you behind bars ever again."

Slim agreed with me that he had to get his life together. He moved into his new apartment but went right back to the drugs, the girls, and the out-of-control partying. It looked like he was just too far gone to save himself, but underneath my anger, I didn't want to give up on him.

Karli and I were still seeing our counselor, and I talked with her about my argument with my father. The counselor pointed out that I was trying to control my father in the same way I'd tried to control my mother for so much of my life. It was hard for me to sit by and watch someone I loved self-destruct, but I was the son, not the parent. I could give Slim my best advice and set clear boundaries for what I would tolerate, but I couldn't cajole or punish him into making good choices.

Then the counselor asked me a question that completely shifted the way I saw my relationship with Slim. "Even if you don't want to talk to your father, can you just love him for him?" she asked. She helped me see that Slim's selfish behavior was a product of his sickness. He had never dealt with his addiction in a meaningful, effective way. He loved my sister and me more than anything, but he was still a prisoner, not locked up by the system, but confined by his own bad habits, guilt, and drug dependency. Her insights opened my eyes to what Slim was up against. It also made me realize that I still had some work to do when it came to forgiving my father.

When the Harveys' camp came around again that June, I told Slim I wanted him there. He was still out on bail, and I thought it would be a positive environment for him to spend time in for a few days. Everyone who met him there the year before had liked Slim. That particular year, I wanted the boys to see my father and me together as I shared our story of spending two decades apart before finding each other and building a father-son relationship. I also wanted Slim to see that, regardless of his fall, I still loved him.

When the day came for Slim to join me at the camp, I called and called, but he never answered his phone. Finally, a woman answered, and I realized he was still at home, partying and getting high. He couldn't leave the drugs alone for one day to show up for me.

I climbed behind the wheel of my truck, drove to his place, and banged on the door on the door so hard that I nearly knocked a hole in it.

Slim cracked the door and peeked out at me like a guilty kid who knows he's about to get spanked. "I changed my mind. I don't want to go. I got company." His bloodshot eyes and slurred voice said it all. He'd been drinking and doing drugs for days. He was a mess. And I was furious.

"I never asked you for one fucking thing in my whole life," I hollered at my father, "but this, I'm asking you. You said you were coming with me, and you're coming."

There was no time for him to shower or change. I yanked him out the door and dragged him into my SUV. The world wasn't running on his schedule. I was on that afternoon's itinerary to speak to the campers, and I wasn't going to let them down.

We weren't driving for long before Slim passed out cold. When we arrived back at the camp, I got out and left him there in the truck. I needed to get away from Slim and get my mind right to address the young campers. I asked the director of the program, Frank Hallum, to deal with my father and get him inside the building as soon as he could. Frank liked Slim, and he had experience with his own father's unpredictable and inappropriate behavior under the influence of drugs. He was kind enough to step in and give me a hand.

What my father didn't understand was that my anger had escalated to such extremes because I had a special reason for having him there that day. In addition to wanting the young men to see a real—life, restored father-son relationship, I wanted to introduce Slim to Mr. Harvey. I had decided to propose to Karli, and before I did, I wanted our fathers to meet. But that plan flew out the window. Slim was in no state to meet the man I hoped would be my future father-in-law. When I decided to postpone the introduction, I didn't know that, in fact, the two men would never have another opportunity to meet.

Slim pulled himself together enough to sit in the audience as I shared my journey with the campers. I described growing up without my father and bouncing from foster home to foster home. I told them how I'd been angry with my father for much of my childhood and adolescence and even as a young man, and I described how I'd found him serving a prison sentence.

When I was done, I told the boys, "My father's here today." I called Slim up to stand next to me, and in front of all of those witnesses, I said to my father, "I love you, Dad. And I forgive you," and we shared an embrace. Later, I found out Slim was angry about some of the things I'd said about him, but I couldn't be responsible for that. I'd told my truth.

I hoped that moment would be an example to the boys, but even more, I so desperately needed to experience it for myself. I needed to say the words "I forgive you" to my father. I needed him to hear them. It was the final step in embracing both of my parents, just as they were, in seeing the good in them, and releasing the shame I'd felt for so much of how they'd lived their lives.

Ultimately, I needed to forgive myself for the anger, resentment, and judgment I'd directed at Slim so I could be free and move on. I knew who I was, Benjamin Raymond, "son of the right hand," and yet still my father's namesake, David Brumfield, and I accepted all of what had made me into the man I'd come to be.

———

Two weeks to the day after that emotional moment at the camp, my father was rearrested. After the first arrest, the police didn't have much on him, but once they had him in their sights, they wouldn't give up. The first time, they'd found drugs in his apartment, but he wasn't there, and when they picked him up, he had nothing illegal on him. It was a weak case. The second time was different.

Unfortunately, once he got out on bail, my father had continued with the same behavior that had gotten him arrested in the first place. His apartment quickly became a party spot, and that made it easy for undercover cops to come in and get more evidence. All it took was one transaction. After that, the police raided his new apartment. They tossed every closet, drawer, cabinet, box, and container. Slim's bail was rescinded, and he was thrown back in jail. The news crushed me.

A couple of my Brumfield cousins shared with me that, just a few days earlier, Slim had called them to say he felt like he was letting

Davida and me down. They could tell he was tired of the street life. He wasn't a young man anymore, and it had all started to wear on him. I only wished those revelations had come to him months earlier.

Karli and I had planned a trip to Seattle the same weekend my father was thrown back in jail, and while I didn't feel like traveling or socializing, I needed to be with her. She had become my greatest confidante and comfort, and more than ever, I appreciated her presence in my life. That weekend with her was exactly the getaway I needed. I needed that distance from Slim and his problems so I could deal with the mix of emotions they'd brought up in me.

As the weeks passed, Slim sobered up behind bars, and he started thinking clearly again. He seemed more like the man I'd first met, and he shared how sorry he was that he'd let Davida and me down. The truth of the matter was that, without the structure of regular drug testing, with no support system or healthy coping skills, he'd gone back to old habits.

He knew he'd messed up, but Slim was finally ready to do the work to change his life. He went through a rigorous screening process and was approved for a structured, long-term rehab-to-work program. It was the kind of good news we all needed, but we had to wait for his sentencing to see if he would be allowed take advantage of rehab. His lawyer wanted him to take a plea for a fifteen-year sentence, but Slim refused. He was optimistic. Slim was certain everything would work out in his favor, but I wasn't so sure.

What I was completely certain about was how I felt about Karli. A couple of months before Slim was to be sentenced, I drove from Dallas to Oklahoma to pick up the custom engagement ring I'd ordered for her. Not wanting to have the conversation over the phone, I'd stolen a moment with her father at a charity golf tournament. His schedule was packed that day, and I'd had to fight to get to him, but I refused to miss another opportunity. The minute I'd gotten his ear, I'd asked for his blessing, and he had given it. With that important tradition taken care of, I'd set my plan in motion.

I had special-ordered a custom ring because I wanted my future wife to have something uniquely hers. Unfortunately, when I arrived at the Oklahoma office, where the ring was supposed to be shipped, no one could find the package. The FedEx representatives insisted there was nothing on the truck for me, but I wasn't going back to Dallas empty-handed. I climbed in the back of the delivery truck and sorted through the packages myself, until finally, I found the ring.

I should have been able to breathe a sigh of relief, but Karli was flying into Dallas to join me for a trip to Punta Mita, Mexico. I'd given her the trip as a birthday present. I planned to surprise her with the proposal on a beautiful Mexican beach, but I was running late to pick her up at the airport. We shared a pet peeve about being left to wait at the airport, so I could not be late under any circumstances. But after my delay in Oklahoma, I didn't see how I could get back to Dallas on time. I started calling my homeboys to see who might be able to go out and grab her for me the minute her feet hit the sidewalk. Luckily, I made it to the airport with five minutes to spare.

I knew Karli suspected I might be proposing soon, so even though I as excited, I tried to appear relaxed and carefree. When we landed in Mexico, we had to go through customs, and I was singled out for a pat down. I tried to play it cool while I whispered to the customs officer that I had the ring on me. Keeping my voice low, I pleaded with him not to blow everything for me. I held my breath, thinking, "If he pulls out the ring, I'm going to have to propose at this airport." He sent me on my way without revealing my surprise. Once again, my proposal plan had been saved.

As we finally collected our luggage and headed to the St. Regis, Punta Mita, I texted Karli's sister, Brandi, one of the few people who was in on my whole plan: "You would not believe what I've been through."

Karli and I settled into our villa, and I told her to take the day to relax. "Friday is your day," I told her. "We can do whatever you want, but Saturday's my day. I've got it all planned out, and we're getting up early."

Karli was not and is not a morning person, but I wanted the day to be perfect, and she obliged me by getting out of bed early. After a nice breakfast and a spa day that included a couple's massage, I told Karli that I had plans for dinner and she needed to be ready on time. "When we get back to the room, you should curl your hair too," I told her.

Karli put up a fuss. We'd been swimming, and she wanted to leave her hair in that casual vacation look. It was a lot of time and trouble for her to blow dry, style, and curl her hair, but it would be worth it. She'd thank me later when she saw our engagement photos.

When she finally got dressed, I texted her father: "It's going down tonight," and he responded: "All right soldier." I felt a pang of sadness that I couldn't reach out to my own father, but that moment was about Karli and me, and I was too eager and excited to let anything ruin the day.

As we left the villa, Karli grabbed my arm. "Lover," she said, "there's a man in the bushes taking pictures of us!"

She tried to point him out, but I pulled her away. "Ain't nobody thinking about taking pictures of you," I told her.

"I'm serious," Karli said.

"Nobody knows you here," I told her. If she figured out I'd hired the photographer to document our proposal, everything would be ruined. I rushed her down to the beach.

I had a private cabana set up for us with champagne on ice, but when we reached the entrance to the private beach, the attendant told us he was sorry, but the beach was closed. Karli must have wondered why it was so important to me, but I did some fast talking, and finally, we made it to the cabana.

Before she could get too comfortable, I told Karli, "Let's go down to the water and reflect on things."

Karli looked at me like I must have spent too much time in the sun that day. "Reflect on what?" she asked.

"Come on," I told her. "It's going to be sunset soon. It'll be beautiful."

We walked down to the water's edge right as the sun began to go down. I stood just a step behind her and began to pour out my heart. "You know, I really love you, Karli," I said. I told her how incredibly special she was to me. "I'm tired of you being in Atlanta and me being in Dallas. I want us to be together, and I want us to make this a permanent thing.

Karli turned around to ask what I was talking about, but I was already down on one knee. I took her hand in mine and over the sound of waves crashing and Karli crying, I asked, "Karli Maya Harvey, will you marry me?"

And she said yes.

———

In December of 2014, newly engaged and looking forward to the future, I sat in that Dallas courtroom waiting for Slim to be sentenced. When his turn came, the judge looked down and addressed him directly. "You have beautiful kids Mr. Brumfield," she told him, "but one strike, two strikes, three strikes. Where have you shown that you're actually going to make a change?"

I heard her say "twenty-five years," and I felt my spirit deflate. As I left the courthouse, I felt completely numb. *Maybe I had heard her wrong. I must've heard her wrong. I heard her wrong, didn't I? There's no way she said twenty-five years.* Even if he did deserve to go back to jail, my father's offense didn't merit that much time. There were murderers and rapists who served shorter sentences. *Twenty-five years? No.*

I headed back to my office, determined to stay strong and power through my work day, but I was too shaken up to drive. I pulled over to the side of the road to take a moment to get myself together. Sitting there alone, I took a deep breath and called Karli. I needed to hear her voice, and I knew she was waiting, praying for the best possible outcome for all of us.

"Slim's going away again," I told her. I gave her a short replay of the events in the courtroom.

Karli was shocked and sad for my family, but there wasn't much she could say. I was just grateful to have someone so loving and compassionate to turn to in one of my darkest moments.

Aniah and Davida would be devastated. They had established a life in Dallas, and a big part of that had been having Slim there with us. There was no getting around it. I had to call and break the news to my sister. She'd gone through losing Slim to the system before, but it wouldn't be any easier this time around.

Davida was quiet as I explained to her that our father wouldn't be going to the drug rehabilitation program and that, instead, he'd been sentenced to a quarter of a century in prison. She didn't say much, but she didn't have to; we shared the same hurt and disappointment.

Prior to his transfer from the jail to the state prison, where he was expected to spend the next two and a half decades, I went to visit Slim. I brought him the socks he'd asked for, and we spoke about his sentence for a while. He insisted he still had hope for an early release, but I couldn't see how it would happen. Slim also tried to offer me some fatherly advice, but I barely heard what he said. It felt like our roles were reversed, and I hated it.

I'd had to step into a parental role with my mother when I was just a boy, and because of her mental illness, I would always have to provide that kind of support for her. Now, I felt like I had to be the same kind of caretaker and provider for my father, and I didn't want to spend the next twenty-five years that way. As Slim droned on about whatever was on his mind, I just let him talk himself out. We had come so far, only to end up back where we'd started. All I could think about was the fact that my father wouldn't be there for my wedding.

CHAPTER TWENTY

Imagination is everything. It is the preview of life's
coming attractions. —Albert Einstein

I was in awe.

The doors opened, my soon-to-be wife appeared in her wedding gown, and everything and everyone else fell away. From that moment, the room was charged with a current of love that connected the two us. I wiped away tears and composed myself. Karli's beauty was just one of many reasons I knew God had smiled on me when he brought her into my life.

Keeping with tradition, it was the first time I'd seen Karli in her wedding dress, and it turned out to be more than worth the wait. She was absolutely stunning as she approached the altar in a long, fitted white wedding dress embellished with hand-beaded lace and a long train that floated behind her as she glided toward me.

Mr. Harvey walked his daughter down the aisle, and I stepped forward to shake his hand as he entrusted Karli to me. His love for her was evident in the tears he shed, and it meant a lot to me that he not only supported us in our decision to marry but had first judged me as a man of integrity, kindness, and devotion—someone who would provide for, protect, and adore one of the most important people in the world to him for the rest of her life.

Along with some of our closest friends, my sister and Karli's siblings stood up for us. Rev. Marvin McMickle, the same pastor who baptized Karli as a child, and under whose spiritual guidance she'd grown up, officiated our ceremony. While we had almost three hundred wedding guests, Rev. McMickle knew Karli and her family well, and he personalized the service in a way that created a feeling of intimacy. Everything was as it should be and even more special than I'd imagined.

Finally, the pastor said, "My heart rejoices to announce that Benjamin and Karli are lawfully husband and wife." As the crowd erupted in applause and Karli and I both burst into smiles, he continued, "And what God has joined together, let no one put asunder. You may kiss the bride." It was the first of many kisses we would share that day. On September 26, 2015, we officially became Team Raymond.

Before our big day, we'd spoken with a lot of married couples about what moments they cherished from their wedding days and what they wished they'd done differently. Over and over, they advised us to really make the day about us and the relationship we would build together from that day forward. We'd taken that advice to heart, and amid all the hoopla, we did all we made sure we never lost sight of each other or the significance of the day. We appreciated every person who came out to witness our union, but ultimately, the day wasn't about hosting our guests or making sure we shook hands with every person at the reception. It was about the two of us coming together as one.

The road to our wedding day had been filled with non-stop appointments and decisions to be made. I made the choices for our venue, the photographer, and the playlist for the reception. Beyond that, I trusted my fiancée to make our day a perfect reflection of us, and she did just that. Because of her father's public platform, we'd shared our wedding plans with his fans and followers for months. In fact, viewers of the *Steve Harvey* television talk show voted to help Karli and me select our wedding invitations, the bakery that would make our cake, looks for my groomsmen, and locations for her bachelorette party and my bachelor party.

When the week of the wedding finally arrived, Karli and I welcomed family and friends for our pre-wedding festivities. For two days prior to the event, we hung out with everyone and enjoyed games, cocktail parties, karaoke, dancing, and an elegant rehearsal dinner, during which Karli's mother gave an emotional toast, and we shared our appreciation for all our parents had done to get us to that moment.

My wife's vision of a space all done up in white, ivory, and gold was brought to life with over one hundred twenty thousand flowers, including white orchids and three different kinds of roses. Crystals and candlelight lent a warm glow to everything, but there was no question that Karli lit up the room.

Karli's father had more than fulfilled his promise to give his daughter the wedding of her dreams. She was delighted with it all, but I had a few surprises for her as well. Before the wedding I'd sent roses and a handwritten card that recounted some of the best moments we'd shared to her room. Before the ceremony began, my best friend also delivered to her an engraved locket with a picture of Karli and me as my wedding gift to her, but I still had more in store for her.

Standing on the dance floor in front of all of our reception guests, I looked my wife, the love of my life, in the eyes and read the words I could only have written for her. I had partnered with J. Ivy, a talented poet and spoken-word artist, to write an original poem to express what a difference Karli made in my life and celebrate our journey of love together.

WHAT DO YOU SAY?

Written By: J. Ivy - Inspired By: Ben & Karli

What do you say to the person who instantly made your life better?
My imperfections weren't judged or measured,
Just embraced and nurtured,
With a face filled with virtue,
Your soul smiled at me and mine smiled right back,
This was a feeling I couldn't fight back,
Fight off,
You caught me with a love hook,
Knocked me off my feet,
Picked me up,
Made me something delicious to eat,
Some nutritious veggie treats,
And I could taste the love in every single bite,
From the beginning our love was right,
It was obvious,
I'm reminded of how extraordinary we are by the way folks look at us,
Our bond is beyond special,
I felt you from the first moment I met you,
There, on June 16, 2012,
At a camp for young men who weren't doing so well,
We were both there to work with hopes of changing their lives,
Who knew our lives would also be changed,
Life would never again be the same,
We spent a little time together and been together ever since,
Together we make sense,
It ain't been perfect,
But through the ups and downs we work it,
We take trips on the weekend cause you're worth it,
We're worth it,
That's why we settled up,
Earned one another's trust,
We step in the spot and turn up,
Turn down for what,

You turn on every desire,
Please know that your entire existence is admired and respected,
I opened up,
Dropped my guard,
And my heart never felt more protected,
I promise to protect you,
You're so, so beautiful,
You make me want to stand up,
Man up,
Dance with you,
Globetrot,
Move from spot to spot so the world can spot our love,
When you need to be held I got a thousand hugs,
A listening ear,
An understanding tone,
From here on out you'll never be alone,
Your mere presence turned our house into a home,
My God I'm blessed,
Thank God you said yes,
Our style moves pass being the best dressed,
Cause you bring out my best,
You're my best friend and lover,
You're the best gift ever discovered,
With you, new levels of joy have been uncovered,
Daily you show me what true love really means,
My Queen, your love is like cool fresh water in the middle of a blaze,
Which is why our days are spent lighting up any room,
We're more than a bride and a groom,
We're the sun and the moon,
Dreaming of the stars we'll create,
It's you I celebrate,
Because what we have is so true,
What do you say to the person who instantly made your life better?
Thank You!
I Love You!!
God Bless You!!!

When I finished the poem, I asked Karli to share our first dance as husband and wife with me. "And I have a friend here who wants to sing for us," I told her.

Karli looked completely confused. She'd planned so many of the wedding details, but not this one.

"Please welcome," I told her, "Mr. Kenny Lattimore!"

This last surprise almost left her speechless, but not before she blurted, "What the—!" in front of everyone. I took great pleasure in watching the shock on her face transform to pure joy as R&B superstar Kenny Lattimore stepped out of the wings to sing his hit song "For You," Karli's favorite wedding song. Once she finished screaming, tears rolling down her face, my wife and I danced together. As I held her in my arms, I looked forward to making every day the day of her dreams.

In the weeks following our wedding, several couples would share with us that the authenticity and emotion of our ceremony had inspired them to renew their commitment to each other, a true compliment and wonderful unexpected effect. Bishop T.D. Jakes, whose church we attended in Dallas and who was a guest at our wedding, told us he could feel the love between Karli and me as she walked down the aisle. We had created a unique and memorable experience for ourselves and for our guests. But with the ceremony behind us, it was time for a little rest and relaxation before we got back to our everyday lives.

After a night of recovery in Atlanta, we traveled to Hong Kong, where we explored the luxuries of city life for a few days, enjoyed the casinos of Macau, where we tried our luck at the roulette tables, and then went on to Bali. The St. Regis theme for our wedding continued. We'd gotten engaged at the St. Regis in Punta Mita, Mexico, and married at the St. Regis in the Buckhead neighborhood of Atlanta, and finally, we stayed in a lavish, sprawling villa right on the beach in Bali. A world away from home, Karli and I lounged by the pool, enjoying each other's company, fine food, and cocktails. We met several couples who had been married for years. They happily shared what they'd learned about making marriage work, and we welcomed the advice.

The kid in me, who grew up wearing secondhand clothes and wishing for someplace to belong, took it all in. The family I'd longed for as a child, I was creating for myself with a strong, intelligent, gorgeous woman by my side. I had let go of my childhood dream of the perfect family, and together, Karli and I were building something real and lasting.

Our fourteen-day honeymoon was the perfect finale to our engagement, months of wedding planning, a special ceremony, and our official commitment to spend our lives together. We'd left behind work and all the day-to-day demands on our time to really focus on each other and enjoy our new status as husband and wife. Little did we know that trip was also the start of another new, unexpected chapter in our lives.

———

For the first time since we'd met, Karli and I were living in the same city. My new wife officially moved from Atlanta, Georgia, to Dallas, Texas, where we both dove back into our business ventures. Karli's work with her father's foundation and the mentoring where she and I had met allowed her the flexibility to work from a new home base. Not long after we returned to Dallas, she was back in the swing of things and traveling around the country for foundation meetings.

My agency had already broken records, but at the beginning of 2015, I'd set a goal that few people thought I could achieve. I wanted to earn a place in the exclusive Million Dollar Round Table, a trade association open only to the top one percent of insurance and financial services professionals in the world. Members represent the best of the best from every company. I'd been away from my agency for three weeks as we entered the last quarter of 2015. No one would have blinked if our progress had slowed during that time. But once a goal is on my plate, I'm not going to quit. I'm going for it full out. I had my team up to speed so they could work independently in my absence, and after my honeymoon, I jumped right back in with them.

Karli made a smooth transition to life in Dallas, but in the weeks following the honeymoon, she didn't feel quite like herself. She didn't have her usual energy, and she wondered why she was feeling just a little off. One Monday, I got up to head to the office after spending a relaxing weekend at home, and she stopped me on my way out the door. "Lover," she said, "I think I'm pregnant."

Even though she wasn't one hundred percent sure, the announcement caught me completely off guard. Immediately, my thoughts raced to whether or not it could be true and what it would mean for us if it were. Where would we put a baby in our small condo? How would a pregnancy affect Karli's health? What kind of help would we need?

Karli was less anxious. "We'll just wait and see," she said.

I really didn't want to be kept in suspense. "We need to get a test," I told her.

We did get a pregnancy test. Karli took it, and it was positive. Less than two months into our new marriage, and we were going to be parents.

We certainly hadn't planned on a honeymoon baby, but we wanted children. Life throws us curveballs, and how we handle them often depends on how well we've prepared for the unexpected. All of the time Karli and I invested in equipping ourselves to be the best possible husband and wife we could be—all of the counseling, deep conversations, and setting expectations—had laid a foundation for us to move up our family-planning schedule and still keep our marriage rock solid.

Big life transitions always come with challenges, but we'd done all we could to minimize the difficulty of this one. We'd already discussed how we wanted to raise our children. Either God saw that we were ready, or we were close enough and he would take us the rest of the way. His timeline superseded ours. We would be parents before we'd been married a year.

As Karli's pregnancy progressed, we shared the news with friends and family, and my excitement grew along with theirs. I was going to be a father.

———

Back at the office, my team and I never let up. We pushed to reach our goal of achieving Million Dollar Round Table until the last day of 2015. Looking at the numbers, I knew we had done it, but when the official announcement was made in January, it was really time to celebrate.

The satisfaction was so much richer when I thought of the people who'd doubted me. The idea that a young agency owner like me could make it to the top one percent of financial services professionals had seemed ridiculous to them. But now, there was nothing the haters could say. They had underestimated my drive and determination to win. The stats spoke for themselves. Top one percent in the world.

My agency had started 2015 more slowly than I would have liked, but we had knuckled down to achieve something most people in my industry would never even try to do. The same drive that had helped me take my high school team to state and win conference championships, the same desire that had kept me focused and on track as I moved from one foster home to another, and the same determination that had pushed me to challenge my college coach for my rightful spot on the team had gotten me the biggest win of my professional career to date.

It was a big deal, and I rewarded my team by sending them out for a night on the town. As for me, I really wanted to celebrate the moment with Karli. When I shared the news with my wife, we laughed at the timing. Million Dollar Round Table membership came with a lot of travel opportunities, but her pregnancy and the birth of our son would mean I wouldn't be able to take advantage of all of it. It didn't matter. I'd done what I set out to do. No one could take that accomplishment away from me.

———

Although I'd built a top-performing agency in Dallas and had created a full life for myself in that city, I could see a potential problem with living there. With the birth of our child, Karli would want to be closer to her family, and as new parents with busy lives, we'd need all of the support we could get. I recognized how much richness and joy a multi-generational extended family could add to a child's life. I'd imagined that, over time, I'd structure my business so that we could live in both cities, but there wasn't time to do that before the baby came, and I wanted the best for my wife and for our son. It didn't take long for me to figure out that would mean relocating to Atlanta, where much of Karli's family lived, as soon as possible.

Transferring an agency to another state wasn't a common occurrence within the company. In fact, it was almost never done. A move like that essentially meant starting over with an entirely new customer base, and for legitimate reasons, it's not something the company encourages. Still, I wanted to give it my best shot, and I started a conversation with the executives about making it happen. Because I knew it could be a long process to get the approval, if it happened at all, I didn't tell Karli about the negotiations I'd entered into with the company.

In her second trimester, she went in for a 4-D ultrasound. It not only gave us a clear peek at our child, it also revealed the sex of the baby. When I saw we were having a little boy, I couldn't contain myself. I was bursting with pride and excitement, and I erupted with shouts and screams in the doctor's office. It took a minute for everyone to calm me down.

Of course, I would have been happy to have a daughter. A healthy baby was my top priority. But having a boy to carry on my legacy and share my name, a name that had come to hold a deep significance for me, marked an extraordinary milestone in my life and the life of my new family. It would have been a great time to share with Karli that we might be able to raise our son surrounded by extended family, but the deal was still in negotiations, so I kept it to myself.

———

As Karli entered the third trimester of her pregnancy, I had the opportunity to travel to Cape Town, South Africa, and London, England, because of my Million Dollar Round Table membership. I recognized that such a long trip might be uncomfortable for her at that point, and in an effort to be considerate, I told her she didn't have to go.

"What are you talking about?" Karli asked.

"That's a lot of hours on the plane, and you'll be away from your doctor and everything," I explained.

"I'm going on the trip," Karli said.

"You don't have to," I told her. "In fact, I could take your mother. She might enjoy it."

That wasn't going to happen.

Karli insisted she didn't want to miss the trip. She was excited for my success, and she wanted to celebrate it to the fullest. Besides, she'd be grounded soon enough. We traveled to Cape Town together.

While we were there, I met with executives and finalized the agency transfer. It was such a relief that I couldn't wait any longer to share the news with my wife. It was Easter weekend of 2016, and I went out and bought bunches of bouquets and covered our table in the hotel restaurant with flowers. When Karli came downstairs to join me, I handed her a card expressing my love and appreciation for her. And then I told her, "We're moving to Atlanta."

My wife was overwhelmed with joy and disbelief. The moment was all the sweeter because Karli had never asked me to make the move happen and she hadn't seen it coming. She was willing to sacrifice and stay in Dallas over the long haul, but if one of us had to carry an extra burden in the early years of our son's life, I wanted it to be me. After all, I'd spent a lifetime learning how to make unexpected adjustments. I was glad to make this one for the sake of my wife's happiness.

The move to Atlanta was officially underway. Karli and I would both miss the personal and professional relationships we'd established in Dallas, but we agreed it was important to maintain our connections there and we planned to return to the city frequently. I'd have to build a new agency from the ground up, establish a professional network in a new city, and acclimate myself to a new and different lifestyle, but I looked forward to the challenge.

I saw Atlanta as a land of opportunity. I'd managed to achieve success in the "old money" world of Dallas, Texas—not an easy culture to break into as a young black man with no existing connection to the community. As far as I was concerned, the sky was the limit in Atlanta, Georgia, a city known for its hustle and entrepreneurial spirit. It was time to pull on my work boots again, and I was ready.

This move was the best thing for our rapidly expanding family, but it would also impact other people, and I didn't want to take that for granted. It would change things for my sister and my niece, both of whom I loved dearly, after they had relocated to Dallas to be near me. And it would completely change things for everyone who worked at the agency.

When the time came to break the news, I promised my team that I wouldn't leave anyone hanging, and before I left I made sure everyone had found new employment. The only exceptions were the team members who decided to make the move with me. Telling Davida and Aniah was more difficult, but I wanted them to know nothing would change the fact that we were family. Wherever I was in the world, I would always be there for them.

When it was all said and done, Karli and I would make the move four months after the birth of our son. Any challenges we faced in that transition we'd face together.

———

"Lover, I think my water broke." Those were the words Karli woke me up with at 3:00 a.m. on a warm June night. I opened my eyes to see my very pregnant wife standing over me.

Karli had visited her obstetrician, Dr. Xercela Littles, just the day before. From the beginning of the pregnancy, Dr. Littles had given us special care, and we trusted her and valued her judgment. When she said Karli wasn't close to delivering yet, we assumed it would be several more days. In fact, at dinner that night at our favorite Italian spot, we'd joked about how late our son would be. "He probably won't come until July," I'd said. But it looked like we'd all been wrong.

It was time to go to the hospital, but since she wasn't feeling any contractions yet, my glam goddess took the next forty-five minutes to do her makeup. She planned to have natural childbirth and had wanted to deliver at a birthing center. I, on the other hand, wasn't taking any chances with her or our baby. Natural childbirth was her decision, but I'd insisted she deliver at a hospital, someplace fully equipped to handle any complications. It was located just down the street from where we lived, and Karli felt great, so we took our time and arrived at the hospital around five in the morning.

The doctor confirmed that yes, Karli's water had broken, and told her that no, she couldn't have anything to eat from that point on. She still wasn't feeling much in the way of contractions, so we reached out and let our family know our son was on his way. Mr. Harvey was out of the country, but I called Brandi, my wife's twin sister, and just after noon, she arrived in Dallas and joined us at the hospital—just as Karli's labor intensified.

Once the contractions kicked in, they came on strong. We tried using the birthing ball and water immersion, but her labor didn't progress as expected.

After Karli had a shower, Brandi told her sister, "All that makeup you did just went down the drain."

Karli waved off her twin with a chuckle, but then she was suddenly serious. "Wait a minute," she said. "Do I smell musty?"

The nurse looked at her and shook her head. "I think that's me. My deodorant wore out hours ago."

Everyone in the room lifted an arm to see if we were the source of the odor Karli had picked up. Then we fell out laughing. Who worries about hygiene after hours and hours of labor? My wife, that's who.

When she was in the throes of intense contractions and still only three centimeters dilated, I was sure my wife would have to tap out, give up the idea of natural childbirth, and take the epidural. I would have supported whatever choice she made, but she hung in there and stuck with her plan.

Karli felt every bit of the eleven hours of labor that delivered our son to us. When she gripped my shoulder and dug in hard, I felt that too, but it was nothing compared to what she endured, and I couldn't complain. The Warriors faced the Cavaliers in game 6 of the NBA Finals that night, but I missed that game. My wife had my full attention.

At 10:11 p.m., our son was born. I cut the umbilical cord and held my son in my arms. Here was a part of me, a life my wife and I had brought into the world. This little guy would be looking up to me for guidance and love and approval for the rest of his life, and I would always be there when he needed me. I didn't want to separate from him for a moment, so I went with him for his tests and slept on the couch in Karli's room with his bassinet next to me.

As I was destined to be named Benjamin Troy Raymond, so was I destined to have a son, my namesake. Benjamin Troy Raymond II, "son of my right hand," came into the world and into my life on Thursday, June 16, 2016, delivered in room sixteen, four years to the day from the day I met his mother at the mentoring camp, the place where I first shared my story. BJ was the greatest anniversary gift his mother and I could have hoped to receive.

EPILOGUE

Ultimately, you are only as good as your legacy.

Our little man grows bigger and stronger every day. BJ is just like his dad was as a kid, big for his age, and while he favors his mother, he looks just like I did when I was a boy. Our son is surrounded by people who love him and will teach and guide and protect him as he grows to manhood.

My wife and I live our lives by the power of the vision. When I look at our vision boards each day, I see the future we're creating together. Karli and I are true partners in our efforts to make our vision a reality. We'd love to add another child to our family, so BJ will have a sibling to grow up with, and we'll continue to parent guided by principles of service, scholarship, mentorship, and faith.

Davida has found new ways to tap into her full potential. She's learning that she can do more than she ever thought possible, including launching her own business as an aesthetician. I'm proud of the work ethic and focus my sister models for Aniah. When you're willing to do the work, anything is possible. They're both discovering that their opportunities are limitless.

I've made my peace with the rough times my mother and I shared. We were once all each other had, and that bond will never be broken. The healthier she is the more she can enjoy BJ, and the more he can enjoy and appreciate his grandmother. I want that relationship for my son. I want it for my mother too. She deserves it.

My mother and my stepfather, Derrel, have found a balance that works for them, and I have also come to love and respect him. No matter what happened in their lives or how my mother struggled with her depression, anxiety, and paranoia, he has never given up on her. Bonnie and Clyde continue to stick by each other through it all.

As I write this, Slim is still serving his sentence in a Texas state prison. I'm so grateful that I found a way to forgive my father and meet him where he was so we could build a relationship. I look forward to the day he's a free man again and can participate in his grandson's life. Just as I used to imagine him showing up for me when I was a little boy, I imagine my father sitting in the stands cheering at BJ's games, wearing a paper hat at his birthday parties, and showing up for Grandparent's Day at BJ's school. Because I love him, I will never give up hope.

I deeply appreciate how far I've come in my life, defying the odds with the help of people who reached out to me when I needed it most. As a result of my journey, there's one thing I know for sure. My son will never have to play this game of life on his own. Along the way, he'll have many great coaches, but none will be more dedicated to teaching him the full meaning of success and helping him achieve it than his mother and I.

For my son, I am forever committed to being the kind of coach I never had.

ABOUT THE AUTHOR

Benjamin Raymond is a former athlete who brings the leadership, discipline, and determination that made him a record-breaker on the court to his work as a business owner, motivational speaker, and a philanthropist. As a transformational coach, Benjamin specializes in helping people and organizations bridge the gap to reach the next level in business, relationships, and life.

Benjamin is the founder of the award-winning Raymond Agency, one of the nation's top insurance and financial services agencies. After working with organizations like NBA Basketballs without Borders, Habitat for Humanity, The Steve and Marjorie Harvey Foundation, the Boys and Girls Club, Urban League, the YMCA, and others, Benjamin was inspired to found the Raymond Family Foundation, a nonprofit organization with a mission to improve the lives of at-risk youth. Because of Benjamin's journey as an only child raised by a single mother, the foundation has a special focus on reaching fatherless boys.

Family is the center of Benjamin's life. He's happily married to the love of his life, Karli, and thrilled to be a devoted father to their first child, Benjamin Troy Raymond II.

To find out more about Benjamin Raymond, visit: iambenraymond.com or contact: info@iambenraymond.com.